Open Distance Education in India

Open Distance Education in India

Expectation and Experience

P. Satyanarayana
C. Sesharatnam

SHIPRA

₹ 995; US$ 49.75
ISBN: 978-93-86262-76-9

First Published in India in 2018

Open Distance Education in India

Published by:
SHIPRA PUBLICATIONS
LG 18-19, Pankaj Central Market
I.P. Ext., Patparganj, Delhi 110092, India
Tel.: +91 11 2223 5152/6152
E-mail: info@shiprapublication.com
www.shiprapublication.com

Contents

1
Introduction

Distance Education (DE) has been marvelously growing in diverse fashion in many developed and developing countries. This is evidenced by the following:

- A large number of distance education institutions are coming up to offer courses at a distance.
- Many publicly funded distance education institutions are set up throughout the world.
- Legislatures of several national and provincial governments are favouring the creation of distance teaching institutions as cost-effective and cost-efficient means of educational provision.
- Distance education has been recognised as an integral and valued component of national education policies.
- The credibility, validity, reliability and utility of distance education are on the increase.

Distance education is called by various names in different regions. Some of them are:

External Education
Postal Education
Correspondence Education
Extension Education
Distance Learning
Open Education
Open Learning
Open Distance Education
Open Distance Learning
Virtual Education
Online Education
Distribute Learning
Independent Study
Flexibile Learning
Independent Learning

Distance education is an umbrella term which describes all the teaching learning arrangements in which the learner and the teacher are separated by space and time. In fact, it is a mode of delivering education and instruction to learners who are not physically present in a traditional setting of a classroom. Transaction of the curriculum is effected by means of specially prepared materials (self-study (learning) materials) which are delivered to the learners at their doorstep through various media such as print, television, radio, satellite, audio/video tapes, CD-ROMs, Internet and World Wide Web, etc. Also technological medium replaces the inter-personal communication of conventional classroom based education that takes place between the teacher and the learners. Communication between the institution, teacher and learners is mainly through electronic media (telephone, interactive radio counselling, teleconferencing, videoconferencing, chat sessions, email, website, etc.) and also through postal correspondence and limited face to face contact sessions held at Study Centres that are set up by the DE institutions as close to the learners' homes as possible.

Distance education has been variously defined. There is yet no agreement on a single definition. A comprehensive definition of distance education is given by Desmond Keegon. Keegon attempted a synthesis of most of the definitions by identifying the following seven defining elements of distance education:

- the quasi-permanent separation of teacher and learner throughout the length of the learning process.
- the influence of an educational organisation both in the planning and preparation of learning materials and in the provision of student support services.
- the use of technical media, print, audio, video or computer, to unite teacher and learner and carry the content of the course.
- the provision of two-way communication so that the student may benefit from or even initiate dialogue.
- the quasi-permanent absence of the learning group throughout the length of the learning process so that people are usually taught as individuals and not in groups.
- the presence of more industralised features than in conventional oral education.
- the privatisation of institutional learning.

Many exponents have highlighted the various phases of development and growth of distance education system. Prominent among them is James Taylor, who identified five phases of development of distance education considering the main methodology used for imparting education at a distance. Taylor's generations of distance education are given in the following table:

First Generation — The Correspondence Model Print
Second Generation — The Multi-media Model Print Audiotape Videotape Computer-based learning (e.g. CML/CAL/IMM) Interactive video (disk and tape)
Third Generation — The Tele learning Model Audio teleconferencing Videoconferencing Audio graphic Communication Broadcast TV/Radio and Audio teleconferencing
Fourth Generation — The Flexible Learning Model Interactive multimedia (IMM) online Internet-based access to WWW resources Computer mediated communication
Fifth Generation — The Intelligent Flexible Learning Model Interactive multimedia (IMM) online Internet-based access to WWW resources Computer mediated communication, using automated response systems Campus portal access to institutional processes and resources

The models identified by Taylor are based on the progressive developments in the field of technology. When the printing press was invented, it helped to print the material and the postal system helped to distribute the material to distance learners in different locations. Similarly, video and audio technologies of second generation helped the institution to record the lessons for listening at the study centres during the counselling session and to broadcast them through radio and television station. In the third generation, the interactive component was added to the existing technologies to bridge the distance between the teacher and the student. In the fourth generation flexibility in learning was incorporated adding a new dimension the learning process through internet, web-based and computer mediated technologies which brought in the interactive online web-based resources for the learners. Fifth generation is more advanced having automated responsive systems and providing access to computer portals of the institution to the learners. It contributed greatly for the learner flexibility as these technologies are always accessible to learners. Taylor's framework helped to understand the different phases of development of distance education.

Benefits of Distance Education

For the Student/Learner

- increased access and flexibility
- ability to combine work and education
- reduced travel time and costs
- more learner-centred approach
- relevance to authentic learning needs
- enrichment, higher quality and new ways of interaction
- acquisition of 21st century skills necessary for the workplace.

For Institution

- attracting global underserved populations of potential students
- improved teaching quality
- support for continuing education
- reduced need for bricks and mortar infrastructure.

For Employer

- high quality and usually cost effective professional development in the workplace
- reduced travel time and costs
- easy, regular upgrading of skills
- increased productivity
- development of a new learning culture
- sharing of costs and training time
- increased portability of training.

For Government potential to

- increase capacity and cost effectiveness of education and training systems
- reach target groups with limited access to conventional education and training
- reduce gender inequality by allowing women to access higher education through distance learning, while staying at home with their families and in their own countries and communities
- ensure the connection of educational institutions and curricula to the emerging networks and information resources
- support and enhance the quality and relevance of existing educational structures and programmes
- promote innovation and opportunities for lifelong and life-wide learning.

Distance Education (DE) occupied special place in the Indian higher education system because of its major contribution in enhancing the gross enrollment ratio and democratisation of higher education to larger segment of the Indian population, particularly to reach out to the unreached and to meet the demands of lifelong learning which has become more of a necessity in the knowledge society.
The major objectives of Distance Education system are:

- to democratise higher educational large segment of the population in particular the disadvantaged groups such as those living in remote and rural areas, working people, women, etc.;
- to provide an innovative system of university-level education which is both flexible and open in terms of methods and pace of learning; combination of courses, eligibility for enrollment, age of entry, conduct of examination and implementation of the programmes of study;
- to provide an opportunity for upgradation of skills and qualifications; and
- to develop education as a lifelong activity to enable persons to update their knowledge or acquire knowledge in new areas.

India has one of the largest Distance Education systems in the world, second only to China. There are several types of institutions offering DE today:

1. National Open University
2. State Open Universities
3. National Open School
4. State Open Schools
5. Correspondence Institutes of Conventional Universities
6. Extension Directorates of Agricultural Universities
7. Distance Education Departments of Technological Universities
8. Distance Education Divisions of Medical Universities
9. Distance Education Divisions of Law Universities
10. Broadcasting organisations
11. Central and State Governments
12. Private educational and professional organisations recognized by governments
13. Private education and professional organisations

Distance education is challenging the tyranny of conventional education system of 10+2+3. It is a very good vehicle for motivated people who want to reenter the workforce or the education system by getting certified. Distance education has wide open entry gates, but tight exit gates.

Year after years, more people are getting benefitted by distance education. The share of distance education increased from 2.6 per cent in 1975-76 to 8.9% in 1985-86 and further improved to 10.7% in 1990-91 and to 20.56% in 2008-09. At present close to 24% of all enrolments are in the DE system and growing fast.

Distance Education System

Year	*Distance Education Institutions*	*Student Enrolment*
1962	1	1,112
1970-71	17	29,500
1980-81	34	1.6 lakh
1985-86	40	3.5 lakh
1990-91	51	5.9 lakh
1995-96	57	10.3 lakh
2000-01	79	13.7 lakh
2005-06	117	18.3 lakh
2009-10	200	36.6 lakh

Historical Developments

Five decades ago policy-makers realised the imperative need of DE in order to expand the base of higher education. With the expanding base at the elementary and secondary education levels, the demand for higher education had increased. The University Grants Commission (UGC) suggested in its report for 1956-1960 that proposals for evening colleges, correspondence courses and award of external degrees should be considered. The Planning Commission took serious note of such a need and in its Third Five Year Plan mentioned the need for the introduction of correspondence education in the country. In the light of the observations made by the Planning Commission, the Central Advisory Board on Education recommended the setting up of an Expert Committee under the chairmanship of Dr. D.S. Kothari, the then Chairman of UGC, to look into the proposal of introducing correspondence courses. The Expert Committee recommended the institution of correspondence courses in view of the greater flexibility, economic viability and innovative methods of imparting education. The committee also suggested that correspondence courses in India should be administered by the universities only and in the first instance, by one University, viz., the University of Delhi as a pilot project.

Thus, was born in 1962 the University of Delhi's School of Correspondence Courses and Continuing Education. Subsequently the Education Commission (1964-66), under the chairmanship of Dr. D.S.

Kothari, also perceived correspondence education as an answer to the increasing pressure of numbers as well as the growing financial pressures on the universities.

The next decade i.e. the 1970s, saw the growth and spread of the Correspondence Education system in India, by more conventional universities opening Correspondence Course Institutes (subsequently renamed as Directorates of Distance Education/ Centres of Distance Education).

The opportunity of access, affordability and convenience offered by the DE system contributed to its increasing popularity and growth. But again the DE system was plagued by the rigidities of the conventional system. The only flexibility was with regard to the larger number of seats. Education was still out of the reach of the marginalised and the disadvantaged. It was realised that unless we open educational opportunities to the deprived, unless we remove the structural rigidities in our educational system, and unless we integrate the educational system with developments in communication technology, we cannot and will not make headway in realising the uphill task of educating majority of the people and of catering to the diverse types of education that a modern society demands.

Against this background the government introduced the Open University system in the 1980s, with the objective to further democratise opportunities for higher education to large segment of the Indian population, particularly those for whom access was difficult or impossible such as those living in remote and rural areas, working people, women and other adults who wish to acquire and upgrade their knowledge and skills through studies in various fields.

The Ministry of Human Resource Development in its National Policy on Education (NPE) 1986 gave prominence to an Open University (OU) system as a means to augment opportunities for higher education and as an instrument of democratising education. Clearly, the vision was that OUs would be different from conventional universities.

Thus, a new chapter in DE system began with the establishment of Dr B.R. Ambedkar Open University, Hyderabad in 1982, followed by the establishment of Indira Gandhi National Open University at the national level by the Parliament of India in 1985. The idea was accented by many states and 1987 and after years saw the emergence of more Open Universities.

The major responsibility for the promotion and coordination of Open and DE was bestowed by the Parliament on the Indira Gandhi National Open University (IGNOU), instead of the UGC, the statutory authority for regulating higher education in India. Thus, IGNOU became a unique institution as it was entrusted with a dual role: of functioning like an Open University by offering programmes of education and training through distance mode and also acting as the promoter, coordinator of the Open and Distance Education system in the country and determining standards in such systems. To fulfill this particular mandate the Distance Education Council (DEC) was set up by IGNOU in 1991 as a statutory mechanism under IGNOU Act which became operational in February 1992. The DEC functioned within the broad framework, and the policies laid down by the Board of Management of IGNOU while enjoying a significant measure of autonomy in its operations.

As per the mandate of the DEC and the NPE 1986, which was revised in 1992, the DEC started interacting with the State Governments for establishing the SOUs in the respective states. As a result of DEC initiatives several State governments established Open Universities. As emphasised in the NPE of 1986 and subsequently Programme of Action in 1992, the OUs adopted a radically different approach to reach the disadvantaged by adopting a variety of media and delivery channels for dissemination of information and knowledge. As a result of this they have been able to make a definite impact on society, and more Indians have access to higher education than ever before.

The Distance Education Council (DEC) took several initiatives for promotion, coordination and maintenance of standards of open and distance education system in the country. DEC has developed guidelines for regulating the establishment and operation of ODL institutions in the country.

In August 2010 the Ministry of Human Resource Development constituted a Committee under the Chairmanship of Prof. Madhava Menon in respect of regulation of standards of education imparted through distance mode.

In view of the acceptance of the Report submitted by the Madhava Menon Committee by the Ministry of Human Resource Development (MHRD) and its recommendations for the creation of a new regulatory body for ODL system, the Distance Education Council of India (DECI). The Madhava Monon Committee also decided that as an interim measure, the DEC of IGNOU may be shifted to UGC.

Subsequently, the MHRD issued an order, dated 29 December 2012, and transferred the regulatory authority of distance education from IGNOU to UGC. Thereafter, IGNOU notified the repeal and deletion of Statute 28 of IGNOU Act and dissolution of DEC on 1 May 2013. UGC issued an order taking over the physical infrastructure of erstwhile DEC on "as is where is basis" and the staff working at erstwhile DEC on deemed deputation basis. This is an interim measure till such time an independent body namely Distance Education Council of India is created by the Parliament.

Pending the establishment of Distance Education Council of India, UGC issued comprehensive regulations for Distance Education on 23 June 2017. This is a bold initiative of UGC. It has included all the facets of ODL system to make the system more vibrant and quality conscious. These regulations lay down the minimum standards for operating ODL institutions. A few important steps provided under these regulations are:

- Setting up Centrer for Internal Quality Assurance (CIQA) to have a comprehensive and dynamic internal quality assurance system for imparting high quality programmes.
- Comprehensive guidelines for quality monetary mechanism. They include governance and leadership, articulation of higher education objectives, teaching quality, programme development, programme monitoring, staff development, infrastructural resources, learning environment, etc.
- The academic audit process is clearly explained. This includes academic planning, its validation, monitoring and reporting and periodic reviews.
- For maintaining the highest standard in examinations, specific requirements/ norms are laid for setting up and maintaining examination centres.
- Territorial jurisdiction of universities are stated clearly. Franchising arrangement with private coaching institutions are not allowed.
- Educational qualifications and other competencies of counsellor in a learner support centre are clearly laid down.
- Specific requirements of academic and physical infrastructure for Open Universities and dual mode higher educational institutions are also specified.
- Quality assurance guidelines for learning material are also specified. Quality standards for audio video material, online material, computer based material, etc. are narrated clearly. Guidelines of preparing self learning material in print and non-print are also clearly specified. Guidelines for the preparation of project reports for programmes are also stated clearly.
- Minimum standards for opening and operation of study centres are also specified. Further, quality standards for curricula and pedagogy are also laid down in this regulation.
- Norms for empanelment of academic counsellor and counsellor session are clearly specified.

- Use of ICT for synchronous and asynchronous learning (Asynchronous learning can be carried out even while the student is offline. Asynchronous e-learning involves coursework delivered via web, email and message boards that are then posted on online forums. In such cases, students ideally complete the course at their own pace, by using the internet merely as a support tool rather than volunteering exclusively for an e-learning software or online interactive classes) counseling and face-to-face synchronised counseling is also stipulated.
- The option to include MOOC courses to the extent of 20 per cent is also included so that the ODL learners get may also get technological advantage.
- Guidelines for Grievance Redressal System are also laid down.

2

Evolution

The origins of today's distance education in India can be traced to the efforts of commercial institutions to offer postal courses in diverse fields before independence. Two such prominent and popular postal courses institutes, which are older than the recognised college and university level courses, are the International Correspondence Schools (ICS) and the British Institutes (BIET). These Mumbai based institutes offered courses in a variety of subjects such as Foreign Languages, Accounting, Auditing, Designing, Architecture, Engineering, Public Relations, Dress Making, Journalism, Beauty Care, Story Writing, Radio Repairing, Business Management and Commercial Art. Though the postal courses institutes were not recognised by government agencies they gained recognition and reputation on the skills and proficiency of their students who were employed in the market.

In the post Independence period distance education in its early form of postal/ correspondence courses began to partly meet the growing demand for greater educational opportunities. In the higher education sector recognised and supported by government, distance education slowly made its entry through the conventional university system. By 1960s it drew the attention of the people who were deprived of institutionalised educational opportunities. Now it has become a valued component of national education system.

Development of Distance Education in Conventional Education System

In late 1950s for the first time in Independent India, the planners thought of correspondence education as supplementary method to meet the growing demand for higher educational opportunities. The Planning Commission in the Third Five Year Plan made the following observation on university education:

With the expanding base at the elementary and secondary education, the demand for higher education has greatly increased over the past . . . . The rapid expansion in the universities and colleges in recent years has led to a number of problems. These have been reviewed in the report of the University Grants Commission for 1959-60 . . . The Commission has stressed that if deterioration is to be avoided, increase in the number of students should be accompanied by corresponding expansion of physical and other teaching facilities. In the Third Plan larger facilities are being provided for diverting students to vocational and technological education. However, the problem is one of large dimensions and even after taking into account these facilities, the number of those seeking admission to the courses of higher education in arts, science and commerce will be large and suitable criteria for selection have to be adopted. In addition to the provision in the plan for expansion of facilities for higher education, proposals for evening colleges, correspondence courses and the award of external degrees are at present under consideration.

The Central Advisory Board of Education in its meeting held in January 1961 noted the observations of the Planning Commission and recommended that detailed study of correspondence courses be made by a small committee before arriving at a decision to start them. Accordingly, the Union Ministry of Education constituted an Expert Committee under the Chairmanship of D. S. Kothari, the then Chairman of the University Grants Commission. The Committee suggested that it would be desirable to proceed slowly as correspondence education was new to India. It considered the kind of educational and administrative problems that might arise from the opening of an alternative channel in which there would be no regular classroom contact between the teacher and the student. Drawing upon the experience of the other countries like Soviet Union, Australia, the UK, the USA, etc. the Commission felt that it would be possible to create and maintain high education standards in correspondence education and achieve economy. The Committee suggested flexibility to be a significant feature of the system.

The Committee observed and suggested the following:

1. The correspondence method admits greater flexibility than classroom education, particularly in the combination of subjects.
2. Many items of expenditure in the regular system of education can be eliminated in the correspondence method. It should be possible to achieve results with economy.
3. Academic standards are determined by general factors such as admission standards, well-prepared instructional materials, easy to understand texts, ample exercises in the application of knowledge, pretested and constantly revised courses, careful correctional and instructional service, invigilated examinations of quality, careful administration and fair marking standards set for passing examinations. If these factors are kept in mind, it will be possible for persons with concentration and discipline studying through correspondence method to become better instructed and educated.
4. Correspondence courses could provide opportunities for persons who have been denied these facilities and are at present in full-

time employment or are, for other reasons, prevented from availing themselves of facilities at colleges.

5. For correspondence courses leading to the first degree, there should be a personal contact between the teachers and taught for about three weeks in a year, preferably on a tutorial rather than lecture basis. Where the teachers and the university running the courses, are not able to run each contact classes themselves, it should be possible for the university to make alternative arrangements with a university of local educational institutions near the residence of the students concerned.
6. To maintain educational standards, it should be necessary to associate top-ranking scholars and teachers in the preparation of courses and text books, "writing the teacher into the text", is a highly specialised work requiring both aptitude and training and implies the collaborative efforts of teachers, writers and editors.
7. The success of the entire scheme of correspondence courses will depend upon the competence, resourcefulness and dedication of the staff that runs correspondence courses.
8. In the first instance, correspondence courses should be limited to subjects in the Arts and Commerce faculties. In later years, Science and Technology could be introduced.
9. It should be possible to organise correspondence courses on a self-paying basis. Per capita expenditure for correspondence courses should be substantially lower than per capita expenditure at regular colleges.
10. Considerable expenditure will have to be incurred in the preparation of teaching materials, if quality is to be ensured and maintained. To do this without making the scheme unduly expensive, it will be necessary to enroll adequate numbers. It would be much better, to the extent possible, for teaching material prepared by one university or several universities on a cooperative basis to be utilised by all universities running correspondence courses.

All the essential conditions for making correspondence education an effective alternative channel viz. flexibility, well written materials, training of staff, contact programmes, provision of study centres, etc. were perceived by the Committee. It did not, however, take into account the difficulties of operating a new system within the framework of existing university system whose rules, regulations, methods, processes, techniques and organisational structures were set up and geared for face to face education.

The Committee's suggestion that a pilot project of correspondence education be started in the Delhi University was accepted. Accordingly, the Delhi University agreed to the proposal and appointed a sub-committee to work out details of its operation. On the basis of sub-committee's report and concurrence of the UGC, the Delhi University established School of Correspondence Courses and Continuing Education in 1962 and started B.A. courses in English, Mathematics, Modern Indian Languages, Economics, Political Science, History and Commerce through correspondence. The response was good and 1112 students registered for BA Part-I course in the very first year.

In 1964, the Government of India appointed the Education Commission under the Chairmanship of D. S. Kothari to advise the Government on the national pattern of education and on the general principles and policies for the development of education at all stages and in all aspects. The Commission noted that one of the major weaknesses of the existing educational system was that it placed an almost exclusive reliance on full time instruction and did not develop adequately the two other channels of part-time education and private study or own-time study. With regard to the part-time and own-time education it recommended that the opportunities for part-time education through programmes like correspondence education should be extended as widely as possible. The Education Commission observed:

"The correspondence or home study course is a well tried and tested technique. Experience of correspondence courses in other countries of the world such as the USSR, Sweden, the USA, Japan and Australia, where there have been used extensively for a long time encourages us to recommend fuller exploitation of the method for a wide range of purposes, There is hardly any ground for apprehension that correspondence courses are an inferior form of education than what is given in regular schools and colleges. Experience abroad and experiments in India have shown results which on balance tend to strengthen the case for correspondence education."

The Education Commission expressed immense faith in correspondence courses in becoming a "method of taking education to millions who depend upon their own efforts to study whenever they can find time to do so". The Commission recommended that:

1. In order to bring education to those who are unable to even attend part-time courses, widespread organisation of correspondence courses should be organised.
2. Students taking correspondence courses should be provided opportunities to meet the teachers occasionally; they should be given the status of recognised students, and where possible, be attached to some colleges in order to enable them to make use of the library and other facilities.

3. Correspondence courses should be supported by well-coordinated radio and television programmes.
4. Correspondence courses should not be confined to preparing students for the university degrees but should also provide agricultural, industrial and other workers such special courses of instruction as would help them to improve production. Some of the subjects in which courses can be organised are landscaping and gardening, architecture, plumbing, diesel engine, drafting, engineering, business administration, building construction and blueprint reading, surveying, firemanship, mathematics, sheet metal, auto mechanics, commercial art, electronics, radio, television servicing and broadcasting, auxiliary nursing, vocational rehabilitation subjects, industrial electronics and automation, dress-making, business and secretarial subjects, air conditioning, heating, refrigeration, criminal and civil investigation, traffic management, hotel management, factory management and executive training, airline training, photography, professional lock-smithing, upholstery and real estate. Good correspondence courses in thoughtfully identified fields of service will create demand for themselves and can help participation by the people in introducing better methods of production.
5. Correspondence courses should be made available for those who desire to enrich their lives by studying subjects of cultural and aesthetic value.
6. Correspondence courses should be developed for the teachers in schools to keep them abreast with new knowledge as well as with new methods and techniques of learning.
7. The Ministry of Education in collaboration with other Ministries should establish a National Council of Home Studies, for the purpose of accreditation and evaluation of agencies which provide correspondence courses, identification of the areas in which different types of correspondence courses would be of benefit, promote creation of such courses through proper agencies, and conducting evaluation and research.

While finalising the Fourth Five Year Plan, the Planning Commission observed that the expansion of universities and colleges and other institutions of higher learning was a striking feature of the years since independence. Enrollment at the University stage in Science, Arts and Commerce faculties has gone up from 0.3 million in 1950-51 to 1.1 million in 1965-66. While during each of the first two Plans, the enrollment increased by 0.2 million, it was estimated to have risen by 0.4 million during the Third Plan. The Commission expected a further increase of 0.50 million in enrollment during Fourth Plan period i.e. 1966-71.

Since India did not have the necessary expertise on correspondence system of education, the University Grants Commission sent a delegation to the USSR in March-April 1967 to study the scheme of correspondence education in the country.

The delegation specifically recommended correspondence courses for teacher training in India on a restricted scale for the purpose of clearing the backlog of untrained teachers in actual regular service and for improving the level of education of trained teachers with varying qualifications. An important recommendation of the delegation:

1. The traditional single channel of full time education was inadequate to give concrete shape to this ideology. Other channel had therefore to be provided – (i) full time, (ii) evening/ part time, and (iii) correspondence courses. Hundreds and thousands of young boys and girls who, for various personal reasons, had to discontinue education at various stages, get their chance for continuing their education to higher and still higher levels through the 2nd and 3rd channels.
2. A systematic in-service training for all working teachers, at specified intervals – 5 years – is an essential feature of the service conditions of teaching profession in the USSR. Equal importance is given to the training of educational administrators also.
3. Many regular pedagogical institutes have full time day courses, evening/ part-time courses and/ or Correspondence Courses. There are a few institutes exclusively for correspondence courses – Moscow Institute of Pedagogical Study with 9500 students. It is also a centre for research on correspondence courses.
4. There is no stigma attached to the acquisition of qualifications through correspondence courses. On the other hand, it is considered a great achievement to complete correspondence courses successfully.
5. It is our considered opinion that the system of correspondence course for teacher training can be profitably adopted in our country, but it should be restricted in its scope. It should be utilised only for the purpose of clearing the backlog of untrained teachers in actual regular service. This system could also be used to enable our trained teachers with varying qualifications to improve their level of education and advance to higher grades in the profession.

Considering the recommendation of the Education Commission, the Planning Commission, the UGC delegation to Soviet Russia and the satisfactory progress of the pilot project of the Delhi University, the University Grants Commission appointed another committee in 1967-68 to consider the questions of expansion of correspondence courses in universities. This Committee made the following recommendations:

1. Correspondence Course should be started only in well-established universities with strong faculties.
2. Duplication of courses for the same degree should be avoided unless there are compelling reasons to do so.
3. The Universities providing correspondence courses should have centres in different places for contact classes. The colleges should be used as contact points and their laboratory and library facilities used as far as possible.
4. Universities providing correspondence courses should have special library facilities for these courses such as multiple copies of text books and specially prepared books for correspondence courses. In addition, there should be a good collection of correspondence lessons prepared in other countries.
5. It would be desirable to organise a workshop on methodology for the preparation of instructional material.
6. The duration of the degree through correspondence should be the same as for the normal courses.
7. It would be desirable that only a selected number of universities undertake to initiate these courses in first instance.

In the light of the recommendations of the Education Commission and the U.G.C. Committee on the expansion of correspondence courses, the University Grants Commission decided to extend the scheme of correspondence courses to other universities. Punjabi University, Patiala was the second university in the country which was allowed to set up a full-fledged Directorate of Correspondence Courses in 1968 to offer instruction for the Pre-university and B.A. (three-year degree course) in English and Punjabi medium. In keeping with its statutory obligation for the development of the regional language, i.e. Punjabi University also instituted an elementary course (Praveshika) and an Honours course (Giani) in Punjabi. This University was the first University to offer Pre-university Correspondence Course. Later on the Directorate of Correspondence Courses of Punjabi University started Postgraduate courses.

In 1968 another delegation comprising the Principal of the School of Correspondence Courses and Continuing Education of Delhi University and an Educational Officer of the UGC was sent to the USSR under the Indo-USSR Cultural Exchange Programme to study the system of evening and correspondence courses in the USSR. The delegation in its report observed that from the structural point of view correspondence courses in India compared favourably with such courses in Russia and these had been organised on sound line with due emphasis on the maintenance of academic standards of teaching and examinations to ensure that degrees awarded to correspondence courses students carried the same value and weight as the degrees conferred on regular students. The delegation felt that although there was much in common between India and the Soviet Union in regard to the objectives of correspondence courses, yet for historical, social and other reasons, it would neither be feasible nor appropriate for us to emulate the Soviet Correspondence system, though we could bring about certain improvements in our system to increase its operational efficiency. The delegation made the following recommendations:

1. Correspondence courses should be run on academic rather than commercial lines.
2. Contact programmes should be strengthened and attendance made compulsory.
3. Necessary incentives such as paid study leave, travel expenses etc. should be provided to the correspondence students.
4. It should be compulsory for students to submit a prescribed number of response sheets.
5. There should be an adequate provision of multiple copies of text books so that these could be given to students on long term loan.
6. Correspondence Courses should be extended to cover new areas and levels of education such as B.Sc. postgraduate, foreign languages and professional subjects in keeping with social demand for such courses, and where necessary these courses may be restricted to in-service people.
7. There should be no duplication of courses.

In 1971 another delegation went to USSR for further study of correspondence education system there. The delegation visited Correspondence Courses Institutes in Moscow, Tashkent, Kiev and Leningrad and observed that correspondence courses in the USSR had helped in expanding and equalising educational opportunities in a big way. Of about five million students enrolled for higher education in the USSR, 40 per cent studied through correspondence courses, 16 per cent in evening institutes and 44 per cent in day institutes. To meet the requirements of such a large number of correspondence courses for students, there were 16 autonomous institutes of correspondence courses and about 500 correspondence courses faculties or departments attached to various universities throughout the Soviet Union. The delegation made very valuable observations and recommendations for speeding up and strengthening correspondence education in our country, some of which are the following:

1. Correspondence courses in India, if properly developed can go a long way in
   (a) meeting the ever-increasing demand for higher education;

(b) in equalising educational opportunities for all in keeping with our democratic set-up;

(c) in providing continuing education to people engaged in different vocations to ensure better output.

2. Correspondence courses in India could play a triple role in meeting the educational needs of the country — first in eradicating illiteracy, second in educating the adult neo-literates and third in expanding and equalising opportunities of higher education for all.
3. Adequate radio and television facilities should be extended to the Correspondence Courses Institutes to enable them to supplement by radio talks and television programmes, the instruction imparted through the printed lessons.
4. Correspondence Courses Institutes should have a distinguished faculty. In order to attract good, experienced and conscientious teachers the Correspondence Courses Institutes will have to offer some incentives such as higher pay scales and staff quarters, and provide congenial and comfortable working conditions.
5. Special efforts should be made to train teachers in the methodology of teaching techniques and evaluation peculiar to the correspondence method of education. The UGC. should organise special seminars and workshops for this purpose. Some experts from well-known correspondence institutes abroad should be invited to such seminars and workshops.
6. Participation in the International Conferences on Correspondence Education should be encouraged. There should be occasional exchange of expertise also between our institutes and some renowned Correspondence Courses Institutes in some of the developed countries like the USSR, Sweden, Norway, the UK, the USA and Japan, etc.
7. Each Correspondence Course Institute should have an evaluation unit to analyse and asses periodically the success of various methods and techniques employed for imparting instruction through printed lesson, radio talks, correction of response sheets and personal contact programmes. The findings of these units should help the institutes in bringing about the necessary improvements from time to time.

By the beginning of the 1970s, the valuable suggestions made by the committees and delegations from time to time to expand and strengthen correspondence education gained wider recognition and acceptance. They also motivated many correspondence educators to gather periodically to discuss the problems and prospects of correspondence education provided by conventional universities through their separate schools/ institutes/ departments. The Indian University Association for

Continuing Education formed about the same time acted as a catalyst for the gatherings of the correspondence educators to generate academic climate in favour of correspondence education.

National Seminars on Correspondence Education

The Association's first major contribution was the organisation of the first National Seminar on Correspondence Education at Mysore in October 1972 in collaboration with the Mysore University. Later three more National Seminars were held in 1976, 1979 and 1982 at Patiala, Chandigarh and Trivanandrum respectively. The first National Seminar was significant in terms of its rich discussions and valuable recommendations. It afforded an opportunity to the representatives of the participating universities to assess developments in the newly emerging sector of education, and to develop a perspective for the following years. The seminar expected reasonable allocation in the Fifth Year Plan for programmes of continuing education including correspondence courses. The Seminar envisaged the possibility that correspondence education could become an effective agent of change in regard to the quality dimensions of higher education. It further recommended that a Joint Committee of the Commission and the Inter University Board should guide the Universities in promoting correspondence education. Such a Committee might also examine the question whether correspondence education should continue to be organised as part of the general programme of existing universities, or should be organised separately as autonomous organisations, either regional or as units of a network run by a central agency.

The University Grants Commission which had all along been concerned with the development and streamlining of the scheme of correspondence courses, convened in 1974 at Delhi a Conference of the Directors of Correspondence Courses Institutes with a view to assess the functioning and the problems of the Correspondence Courses Institutes and make suggestions for their improvement. The then Vice-Chairman of the UGC in his inaugural address said that "Correspondence Education forms a very important part in our strategy for the improvement of standards of teaching and evaluation in the Fifth Plan period. We have, therefore, to take an overall view of Correspondence Courses in relation to education opportunities, not only in the historical perspective and of existing problems, but keeping in view the formulation of long term policies as well as concrete programmes for immediate action. We envisage that in the Fifth Plan nearly 1/4th of students enrolled in higher education will be in the stream of Correspondence Courses".

The observations and recommendation of the Conference can be classified under five heads:

- Scope of correspondence education in India
- Preparation of reading materials
- Future of correspondence education and the role of the state
- Organisational and administrative set up in a directorate of correspondence courses.
- Ancillary services such as radio talks, television, etc.

The special emphasis in the Fifth Five Year Plan on the expansion of programmes of the non-formal education including correspondence courses, obviously called for further development of the scheme of correspondence courses and the UGC was seized of it. A special meeting of the Standing Committee for Part-time and Own-time Education was therefore convened in October 1974.

The Standing Committee after detailed discussion evolved a set of guidelines for correspondence education which were approved by the UGC in March 1975. The main focus in the guidelines was on the maintenance and coordination of standards. The guidelines *inter alia* provided that:

1. Correspondence courses at the undergraduate level should be introduced by only one university in a State except when a university proposes to introduce correspondence courses in a new faculty at the undergraduate level or when the university already offering correspondence courses reached the optimum size of enrolment, namely, 10,000 or for other valid reasons.
2. Correspondence courses should be started only by universities which have well established teaching departments. The academic responsibility for the contents of the correspondence courses in any given subject and its standards must be assumed by the concerned subject department of the university.
3. It should be compulsory for every student enrolled in correspondence courses to return a certain number of response sheets, say 20 every year, suitably spread over various subjects.
4. High priority should be given to the setting up of study centres in areas where there is a concentration of students.
5. The provision of contact programmes should be an essential feature of correspondence courses programmes, in order that the students may have an opportunity to have the benefit of active contact with teachers through lectures, seminars and other forms of discussion.
6. Grants from the UGC for correspondence courses should be earmarked for such items as contact programmes, study centres, preparation of lessons, core staff and library facilities; the ceiling for such grants from the commission being rupees one lakh per annum per subject.

7. Correspondence courses at the postgraduate level should be started only in those universities which have had the experience of running undergraduate courses for at least three years.

The UGC guidelines helped some universities in giving serious thought to their correspondence courses divisions, but by and large they remained unimplemented. Some universities saw them mainly as money spinners and not as agencies for widening the access to higher educational opportunities. This attitude disturbed the heads of correspondence courses divisions of the universities as well as the correspondence students which was reflected in the later conferences and seminars on correspondence education.

The second National Seminar on correspondence education organised at the Punjabi University, Patiala in 1976 articulated the growing desire of correspondence educators to strengthen correspondence education.

Over the years of experience of correspondence education in conventional universities as its component resulted in the feeling that a central organisation in the country be set up besides the UGC to support, strengthen and monitor the correspondence method of education. This feeling found expression in the recommendation of the National Seminars on Correspondence Education held in 1972 and 1976. In fact, the idea of having an apex body for correspondence courses in conventional universities was accepted in the principle by the UGC even before the First National Seminar.

At the Second National Seminar on Correspondence Education, National Council of Correspondence Education was formed (NCCE), with the objectives:

- to promote the development of correspondence education in India.
- to foster good fellowship and better understanding among correspondence institutes in India.
- to serve as a central agency for the exchange of information regarding the growth and development of correspondence education.
- to undertake the publication of literature on correspondence education in the form of journals, monographs, pamphlets, newsletters, etc.
- to organise conferences/ seminars/ workshops on various aspects of correspondence education.
- To approach the Government, the UGC and other agencies to provide funds and facilities for research in correspondence education and various other projects of the NCCE.

The 11th World Conference of the International Council for Correspondence Education was held in November 1978 at New Delhi. Some of the directors of correspondence institutes participated in the conference. They highlighted the need for strengthening and diversification of correspondence education. In fact, the President of the National Council of Correspondence Education who was also the Director of Correspondence Course of Punjabi University reaffirmed the earlier proposal to establishing a central organisation to promote research in institution system and staff development. He suggested: "it could conduct high level research in the special techniques and methodologies of lesson writing, evaluation, contact programmes and communication media relevant to the needs of correspondence course. Such an organisation could also lay down criteria and standards for correspondence courses and review these from time to time. It could thus serve as a watch-dog of the working of correspondence course in different universities. It could also organise workshops, seminars and orientation programmes for correspondence course teachers, and explore the possibility of evolving uniform syllabi and courses of study for correspondence course students all over the country."

In spite of the acceptance of the proposal by the UGC as early as in 1972 and the continuous demand by the Institutes of Correspondence Courses, no central organisation could be established for streamlining, strengthening and monitoring correspondence education till 1985 when the National Open University was established with the role of conducting and maintaining standards in distance education in the country besides the other roles.

Correspondence education did not make much headway during the Sixties. It started growing in strength in the mid-70s when more and more universities started Institutes of Correspondence Courses. Process was such that by 1978, 26 universities out of 114 offered correspondence courses, which were mainly in liberal arts and commerce at degree level. The number of students registered on these courses virtually doubled between 1973-74 (48,392) and 1977-78 (96,231), which represented an increase from 2.10 per cent to 3.6 per cent of the total enrollment in higher education. Unfortunately, a few of the Correspondence Institutes had grown quantitatively and many became unviable in size with low enrollment due to lack of proper planning, monitoring and evaluation. Several of the Correspondence Institutes became quantitatively weak and imperfect. The UGC itself observed several weaknesses in the correspondence courses system. The main weakness identified by the UGC and the others are the following:

1. Most of the correspondence institutes do not have competent and adequate staff. Best teachers are not posted to work in these institutes. As a result, they have low motivation;
2. More than one university in a State started correspondence courses thereby duplicating efforts resulting in low enrolments in many places;
3. Lessons are prepared in a hurry with no regard to quality;
4. Not much attention is paid to the assignments; they are not evaluated, corrected and returned to the students in time;
5. Most of the correspondence courses do not have study centres and personal contact programmes are organised by only a few institutions;
6. Too much reliance is placed on the printed material and latest communication technology is hardly made use of;
7. There is considerable delay in the dispatch of lessons to the students;
8. Bodies charged with the running of these institutions are not organised properly;
9. Rarely laboratory and library facilities are provided and where ever they exist, they are much below the standards;
10. They do not have identity of their own as they work within the university structure. The latter pay perfunctory attention to the former; and
11. Rarely efforts were made to evaluate and check the standards of those correspondence courses. Therefore, their growth and working is haphazard leaving much to be desired.

Institutes of correspondence courses of some universities adopted some features of the Open University system. Open admission policy is one such feature. For example, in Mysore University's Institute of Correspondence Courses did not insist on any eligibility qualification (except an age restriction) for enrolling into undergraduate and postgraduate courses. The SNDT Women's University, Madras University, Andhra University, etc., continued Open University scheme as part of their correspondence institutes. The fast spread of correspondence education, the meagre student support service and lack of innovativeness and flexibility in courses structure caused alarm among educational planners.

The original guidelines issued by the UGC in 1975 were later modified to conform to the changes in the expectations of correspondence/ distance system of education.

The UGC clearly stated, "The objective of distance education is to provide an alternative mode of education so as to enable those with the necessary aptitude to acquire further knowledge and their professional competence. Distance education courses are thus intended to cater for:

(a) Students who had to discontinue their formal education owing to pecuniary and other circumstances;
(b) students in geographically remote areas;
(c) students who had to discontinue education because of lack of aptitude and motivation but who may later on become motivated;
(d) students who cannot find a seat or do not wish to join a regular college or university department, although they have the necessary qualifications to pursue higher education;
(e) individuals who look upon education as a life-time activity and may either like to refresh their knowledge in an existing discipline or to acquire knowledge in a new area; and
(f) in-service persons."

However, all is not well with the correspondence institutes also. They seemed to suffer from certain limitations which have been succinctly articulated by the Committee appointed by the University Grants Commission (Mrs. Vijaya Muley Committee). The Committee has gone into the working of Correspondence Institutions and has highlighted their deficiencies.

1. Correspondence education is looked down upon and is treated as second class system of education.
2. Most correspondence institutes provide Arts and not Science courses.
3. Most of them offer the same courses which are offered in the formal system. As a result, they have the same rigidities with regard to admission and examinations.
4. Most of them use only one medium, i.e., the print, and are not multimedia based.
5. Very few educational institutions in this country make proper resourse allocation to correspondence courses. Even the assistance provided by the University Grants Commission is insignificant and insufficient.
6. There is practically no coordination among correspondence courses within the country as well as within a State, which had led to duplication of effort and wastage.
7. Finally, correspondence institutes in the universities are very weak. They are not given the status they deserve. The heads of correspondence institutes in many universities are not permanent. They do not have much voice in the decision-making bodies of the Universities.

Open University System

Considering the deficiencies of these correspondence institutions, attempts were made to find out an alternative system of distance education which could meet the growing demand of higher education in an economical way. An initiative in this direction was taken up by the Government of India in the early seventies.

In India, the first proposal for establishing an Open University was made in early seventies. The Ministry of Education and Social Welfare in collaboration with Ministry of Information and Broadcasting, and the UGC, organised a seminar in December 1970 as part of a programme for the observance of International Education Year. Inaugrating the seminar, Professor V.K.R.V. Rao, the then Union Education Minister, first mooted the idea of establishing an Open University in India. He observed:

"... It must cover not only the comparatively limited number of university students, but should cover much larger number of students who drop out from the school at various points, the neo-literates, and eventually all adults who desire to avail these programmes of continuing education. . . . The new interesting programmes of instruction, based on modern science-oriented educational technology for students of higher education studying in the Open University should be made available to this much larger body of population which remains outside the so-called university system."

As a result of these suggestions the Government of India appointed a Working Group with Mr G. Parthasarathi, the then Vice-Chancellor of Jawaharlal Nehru University, Delhi, in 1971 to examine the feasibility of establishing an Open University in India. This Working Group in its report submitted in 1975 stated:

"In a situation of this type, where the expansion of enrollment in higher education has to continue at a terrific pace and where available resources in terms of men and money are limited, the obvious solution, if proper standards are to be maintained and the demand for higher education from different sections of the people is to be met, is to adopt the Open University System with its provision of higher education of part-time or own time basis."

The Group recommended that an Open University be established under an Act of Parliament with jurisdiction over the entire country. This Act was to be enacted after consultation with state governments both in respect of jurisdiction as well as the possibility of drawing upon the resources of the existing institutions for furtherance of the Open University. The functions suggested for the University are:

- to offer courses similar to university programmes for the working population and others who are unable to join regular university courses.
- to offer continuing education for the workforce including government functionaries, professionals and other members in the form of special programmes depending upon the requirements of each category.
- to organise special programmes, for housewives, of General Education, Home-making, Nutrition, Maternity, Child Care, Population Education, etc.
- to carry out certain catalystic functions for universities involving non-formal programmes of higher education.

The proposed Open University was to carry out almost all the functions which were prescribed for the National Institute of Correspondence Education by the Institutes of Correspondence Courses of Conventional Universities and their Organisation. The recommendations of the Working Group did not draw much attention. National Open Universities proposal remained on shelf till 1985.

In 1982, the Committee to Enquire into the Working of the Central Universities, appointed by the Universities Grants Commission under the chairpersonship of Dr. (Mrs) Madhuri R Shah made the following observations:

"To satisfy existing thirst for knowledge as well as degrees, admission to formal courses on the basis of merit requires that opportunities for off-campus studies should be created on a large scale, for a great variety of courses of high quality. We already have a number of universities offering correspondence courses; we need to utilise and coordinate this expertise and infrastructure to create an effective system of distance learning. Mass media, such as radio and television, which are already beginning to be used in conjunction with correspondence education, and for which a greater potential is being created through the satellites, should be employed in a systematic manner to enlarge the scope and enrich the quality of distance education. We could create with available know how in software and hardware a highly proficient and attractive system of education for the whole country of which the present correspondence institutes could become focal points. Courses in new fields, particularly in science and some in technology could also be started, perhaps using college laboratories in off-hours and some of the best teachers could be involved in delivering lectures, libraries of audio and video cassettes could be created to enrich both formal and non-formal education."

The Committee recommended that practical steps for creating a National Open University of Distance Education be taken up without delay.

The debate at the national level of Open University stimulated thinking on the subject in various states. In Andhra Pradesh, proposal was made to start an Open University as early as in 1978. In that year Prof. Ram Reddy visited the British Open University and submitted a Report in which he commended the role of the unique institution and suggested a similar institution for Andhra Pradesh to strengthen non-formal education in the State. The Education Minister liked the suggestion and proposed an Open University. But the proposal did not bear any fruit. About the same time Osmania university made a proposal for starting an Open Education College to strengthen distance education. The College was to have full autonomy but the degrees were to be awarded by the Osmania University. At about the time the Open Education College was to be set up, B. Venkatram, who as an Education Minister requested Prof. G. Ram Reddy to submit a Report on the British Open University in 1978, became the Chief Minister. During the early days of his short tenure, the new Chief Minister revived the interest in Open University. In 1982 the Government of Andhra Pradesh decided to establish an Open University to provide "access to higher education to the adult population of the State, for upgrading their functional capacities and improving quality of their life in context of broader social and political objectives and equalisation of educational opportunities and the emergence of a new concept of life long education". To give shape to this policy, the Government appointed a Committee under the chairmanship of Prof G. Ram Ready, the then Vice-Chancellor of Osmania University and based on the Committee's Report, established the Andhra Pradesh Open University in 1982, the first full fledged and totally public funded distance teaching university in India. The Open University formally came into existence on August 26, 1982. The University was renamed as Dr B.R. Ambedkar Open University. The course of distance education in the country would have been different had this Open University not been set up.

Realising its importance and immediate, the Government of India decided to establish a National Open University in the early part of 1985. The then Prime Minister, Rajiv Gandhi, in his first broadcast to the nation, of 5 January 1985, spelt out the new Government's Policy relating to education and announced the establishment of a National Open University. He observed "... Steps are being taken to establish an Open University to bring higher education within the easy reach of all." The National Open University named after the late Prime Minister

Indira Gandhi was set up on 20 September 1985. The idea of a National Open University initiated in early 70's, thus, became a reality after fifteen years. Interestingly the founder Vice-Chancellor of the first Open University Prof. G. Ram Ready became the first Vice-Chancellor of the National Open University. The credit of setting up and shaping the future of two major Open Universities in the world, as Ramphal, the then Secretary General of the Commonwealth, acclaimed in his address to the first convocation of IGNOUin 1985 goes to Prof Ram Reddy.

The establishment of Indira Gandhi National Open University (IGNOU) marked a new era in the history of Distance Education in India. In this connection, the observations of K.C. Pant, the then Union Minister of Education, while piloting the National Open University Bill in Parliament, are worth recalling. He said:

"As has happened in many other countries, it is expected that the National Open University will have positive impact on the rest of the educational system. Even those students who are not enrolled with it will be able to take advantage of its material and media programmes. We are breaking new ground in the field of education today that we are taking a step which is full of promise and great potential.

The objectives of the University are to advance and disseminate learning and knowledge by a diversity of means. Including the use of any communication technology, to provide opportunities for higher education to a larger segment of population and to promote the educational well-being of the community to encourage Open University and distance education systems in the educational pattern of the country and to coordinate and determine standards in such systems..."

Following IGNOU several states in the country set up Open Universities in their states. Thus, there are now one National Open University and sixteen State Open Universities.

3

Objectives

The reasons for setting up distance education institutes are mainly:

- the need felt in many countries to increase the offer of universality education generally.
- a realisation that adults with jobs, family and social commitments constituted a large group of prospective part-time university students.
- a wish to serve both individuals and society by offering study opportunities to adults, among them disadvantaged groups.
- the need found in many professions for further training at an advanced level.
- a wish to support educational innovation.
- a belief in the feasibility of an economical use of educational resources by mediated teaching.

Two situations influence the decision to plan an open university in a country.

The first relates to population and includes:

- large population.
- distribution over wide areas.
- heterogeneity.
- inability to use conventional education for reasons of employment, distance, cost, age, inadequate qualifications, etc.
- deprivation of educational opportunities during school years.

The second situation relates to courses and teaching and includes:

- lack of sufficient teachers for conventional provision.
- inadequate funds for the capital cost of expansion of traditional provision and for recurrent cost of teacher salaries.
- urgent needs for training and retraining courses in specific areas.
- difficulties in coordinating or modifying the conventional provision to cater to the needs of specific target groups.

Venugopal Reddy and Manjulika listed the following factors that led to the establishment of open universities in developing and developed countries:

- to compensate for a deficiency in the number of qualified teachers.

- to provide a more cost-efficient mode of operation.
- to provide flexible programming on difficult, demanding and rigorous subjects of a specialised nature where and when needed specially in remote areas.
- to provide very high quality educational services on an up-to-date basis.

Open University System in India: Broad Aims and Objectives

India has a vast network of distance education institutions. It is the only country in the world which has 17 independent open universities. The broad aims and objectives of the open university system are:

- to provide an alternative cost effective non-formal channel for tertiary education.
- to supplement the conventional university system and to reduce the pressure on it.
- to provide second chance education to those who have had to discontinue their formal education or could not join regular universities owing to social, economic and other constraints.
- to democratise higher education by providing access to large segment of the population, in particular, the disadvantaged groups such as those living in remote and rural areas, working people, women and other adults who wish to acquire and upgrade their knowledge and/ or skills.
- to strengthen and diversify the degree, diploma and certificate courses related to employment and necessary for building the economy of the country on the basis of its natural and human resources.
- to provide continuing and life-long education to enrich the lives of the people.
- to provide an innovate system of university level education, which is flexible and open in terms of methods and pace of learning, combination of courses, eligibility of enrollment, age of entry, conduct of examination and operation of the programmes with a view to promoting learning and encouraging excellence in new fields of knowledge.

National Policy on Education, 1986: Main Objectives

The main objectives of Indian Open Universities as laid down in the National Policy on Education, 1986 are:

- to reverse the tide of admission in formal institutions.
- to offer education to people in their homes and at their own jobs

- to provide counselling and guidance to people
- to take education to remote villages through radio, television and correspondence courses.

Dr. B.R. Ambedkar Open University: Objectives

- to provide educational opportunities to those students who could not take advantage of institutions of higher learning.
- to realise equality of educational opportunities for higher education for a large segment of the population including those in employment, women including housewives and adults, who wish to upgrade their education or acquire knowledge and studies in various fields through distance education.
- to provide flexibility with regard to eligibility for enrollment, age of entry, choice of courses, methods of learning, conduct of examinations and operation of the programmes.
- to complement the programmes of the existing universities in the state in the field of higher learning so as to maintain the highest standards on par with the best universities in the country.
- to promote integration within the State through its policies and programmes.
- to offer degree courses and non-degree certificate courses for the benefit of working population in various fields and for the benefit of those who wish to enrich their lives by studying subjects of cultural and aesthetic values.
- to make provision for research and for the advancement and dissemination of knowledge.

Indira Gandhi National Open UniversityObjectives

- to advance and disseminate learning and knowledge by a diversity of means including the use of communication technology.
- to provide opportunities for higher education to a large segment of the population.
- to promote the education for the well-being of the community.
- to encourage the open university and distance education system in the educational pattern of the country.

Tamil Nadu Open University: Objectives

- to provide an alternative non-formal, cost effective channel for obtaining tertiary education to those who seek it.
- to supplement the efforts of Conventional University systems in providing tertiary education thereby reducing the pressure on those systems.

- to provide a "second chance" to those who had to discontinue their formal education for reasons of their own.
- to provide easy access to good quality higher education to "all" in general, and "the disadvantaged" in particular, by delivering the same at their door steps.
- to provide an opportunity to those who are gainfully employed to upgrade their knowledge and skill tailored to meet specific vocational/ professional needs, whenever they wish to do so.
- to design an innovative system of good quality university education that is flexible not only with respect to entry criteria, but also with respect to what to learn, when to learn and how to learn.
- to design and provide local specific employment oriented programmes.

Directorate of Distance Education of Maulana Azad National Urdu University: Aims

- to develop love for Urdu in the hearts of non-Urdu speaking people and kindle in them a desire to learn the language.
- to reach the unreached.
- to carry the education opportunities to the door step of learners.
- to light the lamp of information, knowledge and wisdom in every home and every mind.
- to develop and promote higher standards of excellence in education.
- to cater to poor and other under-privileged persons of society.
- to enable people to learn at their place, pace and time.
- to cater to the employed people who cannot attend a formal schedule of instructions.

Centre for Distance Education of Potti Sriramulu Telugu University, Hyderabad: Aims

- to provide access to higher education for the larger sections of the population particularly the disadvantaged groups, employees, house wives living in rural areas of Andhra Pradesh.
- to upgrade or acquire the knowledge and skills of the learner.
- to provide the new methods of educational system at the University level which is open and flexible.
- to introduce the programmes (UG, PG Diploma and Certificate) which are relevant, provide employment opportunities and maintain the rich culture of the country based on the resources available.

- to provide the education and training and to undertake research in various fields of Telugu through Distance Education.
- to provide and design special programmes to meet the needs of the specific groups.

PGRR Centre for Distance Education of Osmania: Aims

- to provide high quality education with minimum expenditure.
- to provide higher educational opportunities to the people who were deprived of the same earlier.
- to meet the challenges of a changing society.
- to extend co-operation and guidance to the learners in all academic matters.
- to design programmes to meet the needs of the learners.
- to associate with other Distance Education Centres and share experience for mutual benefit.
- to equip the learners for the university examinations.

4

Organisation

Distance education institutions with similar goals can be organised in different ways, reflecting philosophical, social, cultural, political, geographical, historical and technological differences of the countries. The research findings on organisational design point towards a continuous process of evolution of the structure as the scope of activities of the institution expands in terms of its concept as well as geographical coverage. Therefore, there is no one optimal structure design which would always serve a strategy with maximum efficiency and effectiveness. However, it would be advisable for an institutional planner to keep the following factors in mind while deciding about the institutional structure:

- it must encourage innovation on the part of academics, staff, students and all the other associates.
- it must serve the institutional objectives both in the short and long run.
- it must facilitate the institutional communication process both within and outside with various interest groups.
- it must contribute towards organisational climate by encouraging participation rather than isolation, between the various officials and academics, and between the institution and the outside world.
- it should facilitate decision making and various implementation processes.
- it must fulfill the aspiration for professional growth of officials and academics, and
- it must provide for task role clarity for various agencies and top officials involved in the implementation. The stability of top-level leadership is also an essential requirement of the structuring process.

Several writers proposed model organisational structures of distance education system.

Planning, Organisation and Management

Whenever a new distance education system is planned, the following questions need to be considered:

- What purposes will it serve? (objectives)
- Who will enroll?(students)
- What courses will be offered? (courses)
- What teaching material and equipment will be used? (media)
- Who will prepare the courses and how? (course creation)
- Who will physically produce and distribute the study material to the students? (physical course production and distribution)
- How will the performance of the students be assessed? (assessment and examinations)
- Who will be responsible for the administration of the system? (administrative)
- How will the system be organisaend managed? (organisation and management)

All these questions seem to have not been considered while planning BRAOU, the first OU in India.

The Report of the Committee on the Establishment of Open University was submitted to the State Government within a period of less than three months of its constitution. The Bill for the establishment of the University was prepared in about a week. It was processed by various Departments of State Government with lightning speed. Then the Bill was passed by the two Houses of the State Legislature in just two days and on the third day the Bill received the assent of the State Governor. A day after, the University was formally inaugurated (26 August 1982). By the time it was inaugurated there was no Vice-Chancellor or staff appointed for the University. The first Vice-Chancellor was later appointed (18 November 1982). All this explains the haste with which the New University came into being. In the absence of a planning committee, no details of the new university could be worked out. From the inception the University faced rough weather.

As stated by the one who was associated with the University:

"The University was established by the Congress Government in August 1982, the Congress Party was defeated at the polls in December, 1982. The newly formed Telugu Desam Party (TDP), headed by a very popular film actor, N .T. Rama Rao, came to power. Since the TDP had come to power for the first time, they started looking critically at all the institutions which were set up during the last few months of the Congress regime. In fact, the Chief Minister declared that he would wind up all those institutions which were set up by the Congress Party during the previous year. Even though APOU was not included in the list of institutions to be wound up, there was a lot of uncertainty about its future."

Thus, amidst uncertainty of its existence and without proper planning of future development India's, first Open University started its journey.

The organisation and management of the new university were to be different from the conventional university. But the policy makers desired that the pattern of management should be broadly similar to that of conventional universities, for any change would create problems in other universities. Therefore the management pattern of the Open University was made more or less similar to other universities in the State with a few changes necessary for effective operation of the University.

The organisational system of an Open University should be different from that of a conventional structure. A number of distance educators and writers proposed model organisational structures for a distance teaching university. The founder Vice-chancellor of BRAOU suggested certain aspects to be taken into consideration in devising an organisational structures for an Indian Open University:

- distance education institutions have academic as well as industrial characters. The organisational structure must cater to both. But there is a possibility that such a situation may lead to friction because the cultures of these two units are different from each other.
- organisational structure should be such as to ensure sufficient autonomy to the distance education institution. There should be decision-making bodies within the distance education institution which have the authority to take all decisions relating to the system.
- the various aspects of distance education work such as registration, records, evaluation, academic affairs, educational technology, educational services, documentation information, finances and planning need to be organised as distinct units with operational freedom closely coordinated.
- the academic work is to be done at the departmental and the school levels. Whether there should be discipline-based departments or not is a matter for the distance education institution to decide. It can be argued that most of the programmes of distance education are inter-disciplinary in nature. Therefore, only the school set up would be useful in such situations.
- for the distance education programme to be strong, some face-to-face instruction needs to be provided. This would involve organising Study Centres/ Regional Centres which will provide facilities for face-to-face interaction between the tutor and students. Such centers need to be organised at convenient places. The tutors/ counsellors have to be attached to these centres. In addition to tutorial facilities, the Study Centres should provide counselling, library and audiovisual facilities. For science and technology students, it is necessary to provide laboratory facilities.

Prof. Ram Reddy, the founder VC of BRAOU also suggested factors which should condition the organisational pattern of an Open University:

- it must encourage innovation on the part of academics, staff, students and all the other associates.
- it must service the institutional objectives both in the short and long run.
- it must facilitate the institutional communication process both within and outside with various interest groups.
- it must contribute towards organisational climate by encouraging participation, rather than isolation, between various officials and academics, and between the institution and the outside world.
- it should facilitate decision-making and various implementation processes.
- it must fulfill the aspirations for professional growth of officials and academics.
- it must provide for task and role clarity for various agencies and top officials involved in the implementation. The stability of top-level leadership is also an essential requirement of the structuring process.

A close look at the structure and processes of BRAOU would indicate the following as observed by Kulandai Swamy and Pillai:

- The Executive Council as the main executive body performs the administrative, financial and managerial functions and not any function which is purely academic.
- The powers and functions of the Planning and Monitoring Board are not specified beyond indicating what its name suggests. This body's composition is completely out of tune with its function.
- The powers of the Academic Senate are absolute and are not shared by any authority including the Executive Council.
- The academic authorities of the University i.e. Academic Senate, Planing and Monitoring Board and Boards of Studies have not been meeting regularly.
- Centralisation of administrative and financial powers in senior officers. Inadequate decentralisation and delegation of powers.
- Positions of Director are part-time.
- Administration and Accounts Manual, which is a compilation of various instructions and resolutions of the Executive Council on different subjects, approval by the Executive Council in 1992 is the only guiding document for the University.

- Complex procedure for registration of students for 2nd and 3rd years of undergraduate studies.
- Absence of academic calendar and schedule of operations.
- No clarity on the role and responsibility of Regional Centres.
- Lack of clarity on the staffing pattern at Headquarters and at Regional and Study Centres.
- Examination schedules are not adhered to, results are not declared in time and marks are not available to students in time.
- Too many structures with too few people to make them effective and fully functional.
- Non-availability of senior academics to the faculties for providing leadership.
- Absence of proper coordination among functional areas as well as officers.
- Staff strength has not increased in proportion to the increase in the volume of the work.
- Even in areas which are purely technical and professional, such as audio/ video products and computing, there are no technical staff.
- No hierarchy in several functional areas, middle level positions are not available.
- No work culture, staff morale is low and no motivation for performance.
- No performance appraisal system, no *incentive* for good performance.
- No policy for transferring people and resistance to transfers.
- Even for decentralised operations, decision-making is centralised.
- Financial management is highly centralised.
- Observance of rules gets precedence over results. Approval processes are cumbersome.

Organisational Structure of BRAOU

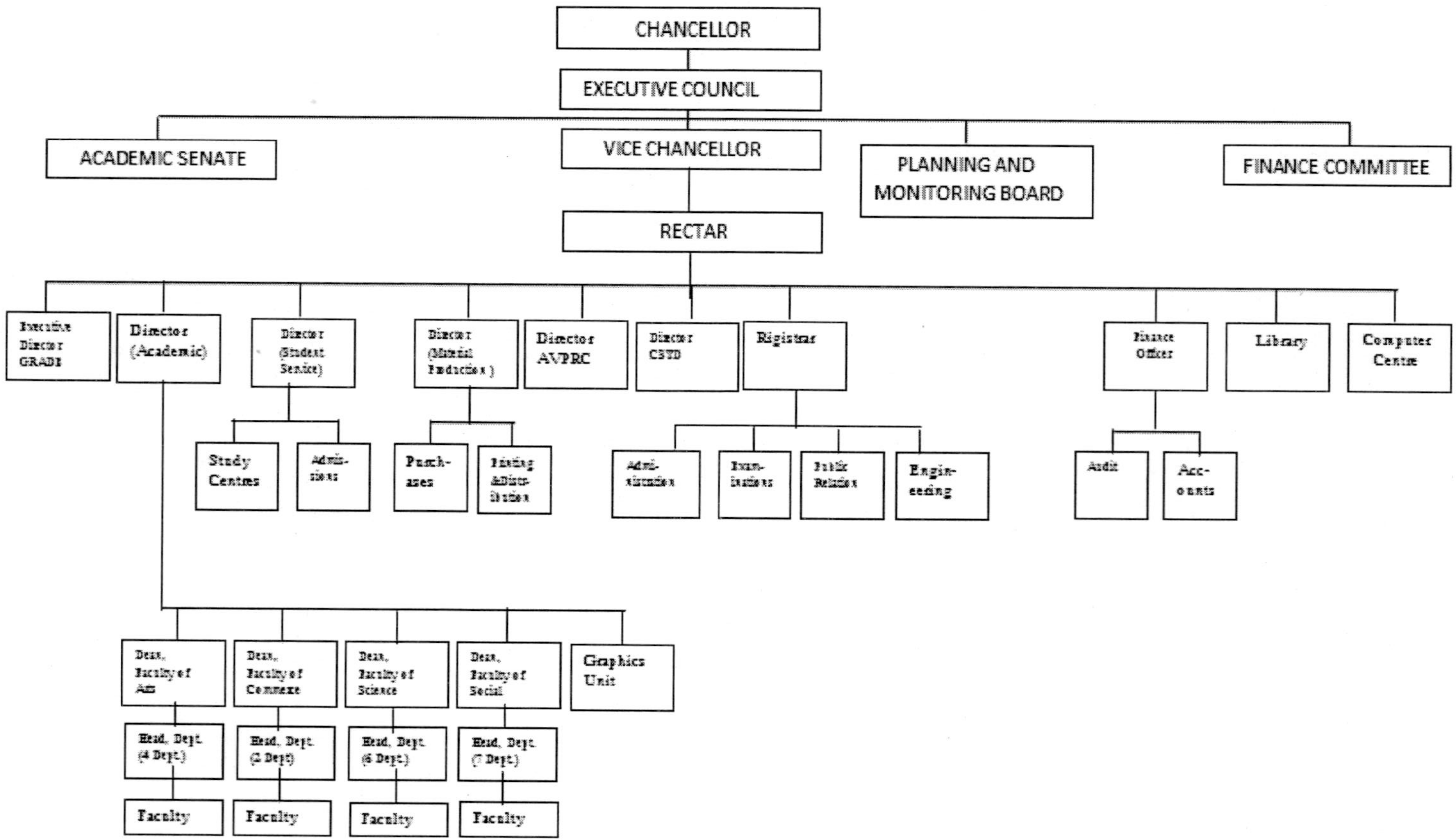

Organisational Structure of Indira Gandhi National Open University

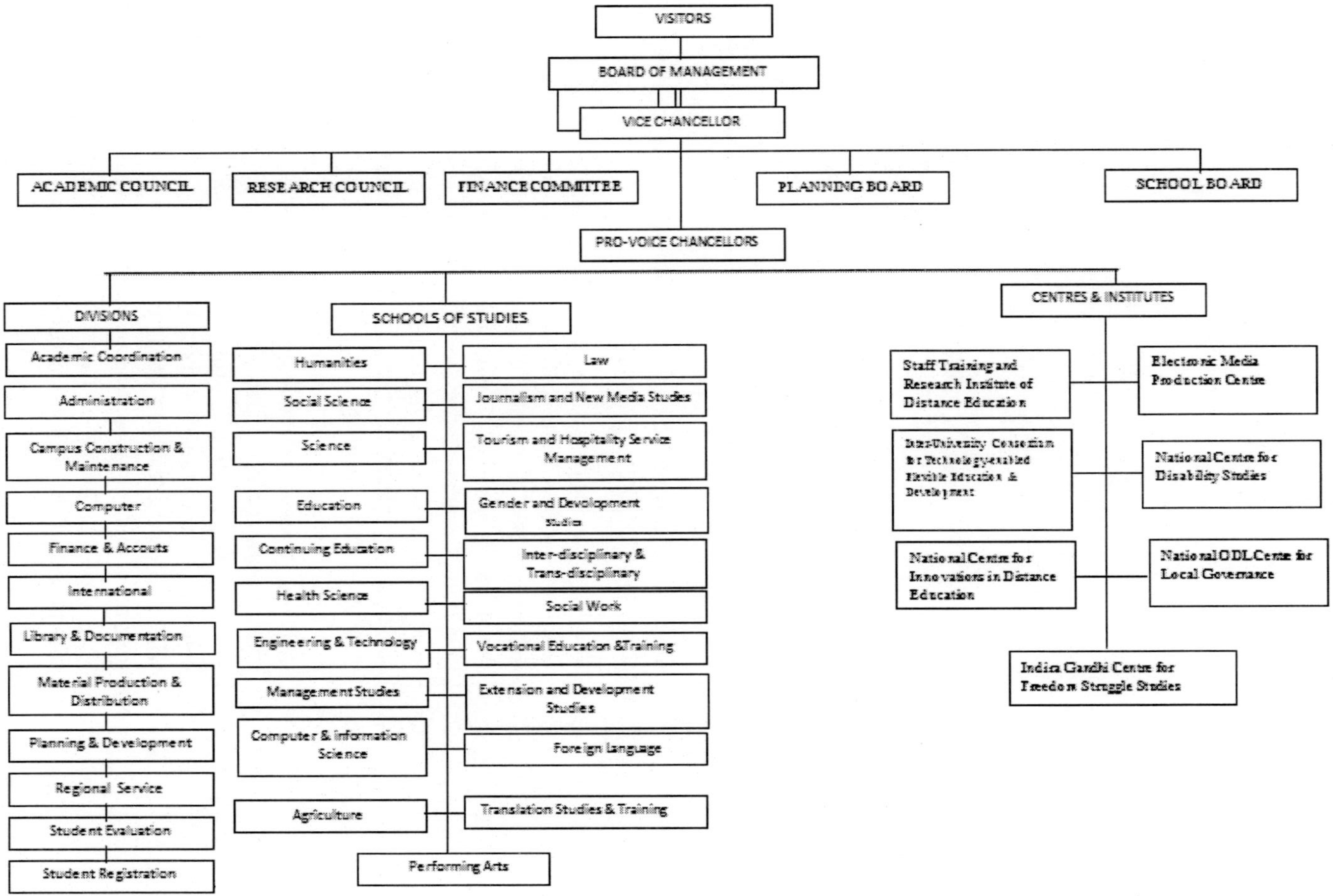

5

Courses

A conventional university or a college, when newly set up, would not experience any difficulty in launching academic programmes. It simply borrows or adopts the programmes of the previously established institutions. Normally, there is no need or scope for any experimentation or innovation.

A distance teaching institution, particularly higher level one, comes into existence not to duplicate the courses run by other traditional institutions. Its aim, goal, purpose and functions are different from a conventional institution. It has to foster and promote the educational development of a community in which it is located. Different sections of the community have different types of educational aspirations and needs. It has to educate the people who remain uneducated due to a variety of reasons — economic, social, cultural and historical. Distance teaching institution has a mandate different from that of conventional one.

The aims of higher distance education institutes reflect the types of distance education they offer. The aims are:

- to offer real educational opportunities at the higher education level to students from different socio-economic classes in the society and especially to adults and those members of the working population who have not previously had the opportunity to attend a traditional institution.
- to meet in part the social demand for higher education at a standard not inferior to those of the best higher educational institutions in the country.
- to contribute to the autonomous development of the country by meeting its needs for trained human resources, particularly in scientific and technological fields.
- to establish institutional structures and processes capable of continuous development and of incorporating innovations that will optimise the teaching learning process.
- to develop a teaching-learning system relevant to the conditions, needs and aspirations of its students, and conducive to the stimulation of the students capacity for creativity and critical thinking.
- to support the development needs of the nation in collaboration with other relevant agencies and institutions.

- to contribute to a significant diminution of unit costs in higher education.
- to provide its educational programmes throughout the country.
- to optimise the productive use of free time by persons following its programmes.

Considerations for Distance Programmes

The academic programmes offered by distance teaching institutes reflect both the underlying philosophies that brought them into existence and determine in part the kinds of students they attract. The following four considerations are particularly important in the academic planning of the distance teaching institutes:

- The demand for trained personnel.
- Human capital theory.
- The liberal Arts tradition.
- The concern with lifelong learning.

Types of Distance Programmes

Academic programmes offered by distance teaching institutes particularly, higher one, are differently categorised by different distance educators. One classification is:

- Academic Programmes: These are normally degree level courses. Many students enrol in these courses because of their need and desire for formal academic qualifications, either for personal reasons or employment changes.
- Vocational Programmes: Students enrol in these courses for specific job related reasons.
- Recreational Programmes: These do not aim at specific vocational needs and do not lead to marketable qualifications. But they aim at specific needs.
- Basic Literacy and Numeracy programmes: These are aimed at developing literacy among adults.

A former Pro-Vice-Chancellor of the UKOU, Ralph Smith classified distance courses into six broad categories:

- Training courses.
- Awareness courses.
- Updating courses.
- Academic courses.
- Conversion courses.
- Upgrading courses.

A former Vice-Chancellor of IGNOU, categorised the courses offered by an open university under six broad heads:

- Programmes that have no comparable courses in conventional institutions (Non-conventional programmes).
- Programmes of specific job relevance/job-orientation (Job-oriented programmes).
- Programmes of specific social-welfare orientation (Welfare-oriented programmes).
- Programmes seeking to cater to the unfulfilled or newly developed aspirations which may or may not have any immediate job-relevance to the learners (Programmes of life long education).
- Programmes seeking to update/upgrade the skills and qualifications of professionals and others with the focus set on an immediate Job-oriented objective (Programmes of Continuing Education).
- Programmes of offer for wider options of those within conventional system (Open Programmes for Conventional students).

Different Levels and Types of Courses

Distance Education Institutes in India offer different levels and types of courses. Some of them are given here.

Indira Gandhi National Open Universities (IGNOU)

IGNOU is offering 228 academic, professional, vocational, awareness generating and skill oriented programmes of study at the level of Certificate, Diploma, Bachelor's Degree, Master's Degree and Doctoral Degree through its Schools of Studies. There are a number of new programmes under development. The focus of the programmes is to meet the various academic and employment needs of the people, especially of the disadvantaged sections of society. A number of programmes have been designed to meet the requirements of continuing education and training of employed people for professional growth. The academic programmes are designed and developed by the faculty in active collaboration with eminent experts from all over the country, NGOs, international oganisations, and in-house instructional designers and media specialists. By providing good quality learning materials (based on sound principles of instructional design) to learners, the University has succeeded in raising the standards of higher education in the country. The University, with its stress on learner-centric education, has introduced a number of modular programmes in order to provide a more flexible learning environment. As a new initiative towards flexible education the university has plans to offer Choice Based Credit system (CBCS) in its Programmes.

All academic programmes have been assigned credit weightage. In terms of study time for learners, one credit is equivalent to 30 hours of study. In general, two-year master's degree programmes are assigned 64 to 72 credits, three-year bachelor's degree programmes are assigned 96 to 124 credits. One year diploma programmes are of 24 to 32 credits and six-month certificate programmes are of 12 to 18 credits. IGNOU provides considerable flexibility in entry qualifications, place, pace and the duration of study. Learners enrolled at other Universities can also join IGNOU programmes simultaneously. Additionally, the learners enrolled in degree programmes in IGNOU can pursue other certificate programmes of the University simultaneously.

IGNOU focuses on research in all the academic disciplines as well as in systemic research about the open and distance learning system. There are several Ph.D./ M. Phil. programmes in place. The University is in collaboration with different organisations for design, development and delivery of its academic programmes e.g., Commonwealth of Learning, World Health Organisation, World Intellectual Property Organisation, various ministries of the Government of India, and the Indian Council of Agricultural Research among others. The University is working for a dedicated platform and mechanism for delivery of online programmes.

IGNOU is the national coordinator for five Swayam Prabha channels: Agriculture, Humanities and Liberal Arts, State Open Universities, Culture and Teacher Education.

There are 21 schools of studies, which are responsible for planning, designing, developing and coordinating the academic progammes and courses offered by the University.

The 21 schools responsible for 228 courses are the following:

1. School of Agriculture
2. School of Computer and Information Science
3. School of Continuing Education
4. School of Education
5. School of Engineering and Technology
6. School of Extension and Development Studies
7. School of Foreign Languages
8. School of Gender and Development Studies
9. School of Health Science
10. School of Humanities
11. School of Inter – Disciplinary and Trans – Disciplinary Studies

12. School of Journalism and New Media Studies
13. School of Law
14. School of Management Studies
15. School of Performing and Visual Arts
16. School of Sciences
17. School of Social Sciences
18. School of Social Work
19. School of Translation Studies and Training
20. School of Tourism, Hospitality Services Management
21. School of Vocational Education and Training.

Courses offered by Dr. B.R. Ambedkar Open University

I	Under Graduate Programmes
II	Masters' Degree Programmes
	M.A. Economics
	M.A. History
	M.A. Public Administration
	M.A. Political Science
	M.A. Sociology
	M.A. Psychology
	M.A. Mass communication and Public Relations
	M.A. Telugu
	M.A. English
	M.A. Hindi
	M.A. Urdu
	M.Sc. Mathematics
	M.Sc. Botany
	M.Sc. Zoology
	M.Sc. Physics
	M.Sc. Chemistry
	M.Sc. Environmental Science
	M.B.A.
	M.B.A. (H.C.M)
	M.Com
III	Professional Programmes (Post Bachelors Level)
	M.L.l.Sc.
	B.L.l.Sc.

	B.P.R.
	B.Ed.
	B.Ed. (special Education)
	M.Sc. Psychology
	M.Ed.
IV	Post Graduate Diploma Programmes
V	Certificate Programmes

Nalsar University of Law

Nalsar University of Law, Hyderabad offers four one year Distance Education Programmes:

1. P.G. Diploma in Patents Law
2. P.G. Diploma in Cyber Laws
3. P.G. Diploma in Media Laws
4. P.G. Diploma in International Humanitarian Law

Symbiosis Centre for Distance Learning

The centre offers the following industry's most recognised distance learning programmes:

MANAGEMENT

- PG Diploma in Business Administration
  (Spl: Marketing/Finance./HR/Operations/CRM/Management Accounting)
- PG Diploma in International Business/ IT Management/ Banking and Finance/ HRM Insurance Management/ Retail Management/ CRM/ SCM/ EXIM
- Certificate in Management Accounting
- Certificate in Entrepreneurship Development
- Certificate in Digital Marketing (4 Months)
  CORPORATE PROGRAMME
  (Learn while you Earn)
- Corporate PG Diploma in Business Administration

LAW

- PG Diploma in Business and Corporate Laws
- Certificate in Cyber Law

INFORMATION TECHNOLOGY

- PG Diploma in Technical Writing

EDUCATION, HUMANITIES AND SOCIAL SIENCES

- PGD in Instructional Design
- PGD in Pre-Primary Teachers' Training
- Diploma in Creative Writing in English
- Diploma in English Language Teaching

National Law School of India University

Distance Education Department (Bangalore) of NLSIU offers the following courses:

1. Two-year Master of Business Laws (MBL) Programme
2. One-year Post Graduate Diploma Courses:
   a) Human Rights Law (PGDHRL)
   b) Medical Law and Ethics (PGDMLE)
   c) Environmental Law (PGDEL)
   d) Intellectual Property Rights Law (PGDIPRL)
   e) Child Rights Law (PGDCRL)
   f) Consumer Law and Practice (PGDCLP)
   g) Cyber Law and Cyber Forensics (PGDCLCF)

Tamil Nadu Open University

The University offers the following programmes:

1. Research Programmes – 12
2. Post Graduate Programmes – 13
3. Under Graduate Programmes – 13
4. Diploma and Certification Programmes – 9
5. Vocational Educational Programmes – 9
6. Off Campus Programme – 8
7. B.Ed Programmes – 1

Osmania University

Prof. G. Ram Reddy Centre for Distance Education of Osmania University offers the following courses.

M.B.A.
M.C.A.
M.A. (Urdu/Hindi/Telugu/Sanskrit/English)
M.A. (Philosophy/Sociology/Public Personnel Mgt.)
M.A. (Economics/Pol. Science/History/ Psychology)

M.Com
M.Sc. (Mathematics)
M.Sc. (Statistics)
B.A. **B.A.** (Mathematics and Statistics)
B.Com (General)
B.B.A.
P.G. Diploma in Mathematics
P.G. Diploma in English Language Teaching
P.G. Diploma in Business Management
P.G. Diploma in Bioinformatics
P.G. Diploma in Computer Applications

Annamalai University

Directorate of Distance Education of the University offers the following programmes:

1. Preparatory Programme
2. Pre-Foundation Programme
3. Under Graduate Programme
4. Law Programme
5. Health Science Programmes
6. Music and Dance Programme
7. Yoga related Programme
8. Library Science Programme
9. P.G. Diploma and Certificate Programme
10. Certificate Programme
11. IT Programme
12. M.B.A. Programme
13. Double Degree Programme

Mukta Swadhyay Peetham of Rashtriya Sanskrit Sansthan.

The Peetham offers the following courses:

1. Prak Shastri Bridge
2. Prak Shastri
3. Shastri Bridge
4. Shastri
5. Acharya Bridge
6. Acharya

7. Sanskrit Journalism Certificate
8. Pali Certificate
9. Prakrit Certificate
10. Pali Elementary
11. Prakrit Elementary

Rashtriya Sanskrit Vidyapeetha

Directorate of Distance Education of Rashtriya Sanskrit Vidyapreetha offers the following programmes:

1. Certificate in Sankrit
2. Diploma in Sanskrit
3. P.G. Diploma in Yoga Vignan
4. Pre Sastri
5. Sastri
6. B.A. Sanskrit
7. Acharya

Indian Board of Alternative Medicines

The Board offers the following two distance education programmes:

1. Bachelor of Alternative System of Medicines
2. M.D. in Alteranative Medicines

Institute of Rail Transport.

The Institute offers the following one year Diploma Courses by correspondence:

1. Multi Model Transport and Logistics and Management.
2. Rail Transport and Management.

Tamil Nadu Agricultural University

PG Degree Courses – Two years

- Master of Business Administration
- MBA (Rural Banking and Finance Management)
- M.Sc. (Environmental Management)
- M.Sc. (Sugarcane Technology)

PG Diploma Courses – One year

- Bioinformatics
- Food Biotechnology
- Food Science and Processing
- Energy Management
- Production and Quality control in Medicinal Plants

Farm Science Courses

- B.Farm Science– Three years
- M.Farm Science– Two years

Diploma Courses

- Diploma in Agri-inputs

Certificate Courses:

- Sugarcane Production Technology
- Nursery Techniques and Propagation of Horticultural Plants
- Mushroom Production
- Preservation of Fruits and Vegetables
- Repair and Maintenance of Farm Equipments and Machineries
- Waste Recycling and Vermi Composting
- Bee Keeping
- Coconut Cultivation Technology
- Cotton Cultivation Technology
- Bakery and Confectionary Products
- Organic Farming
- Sericulture
- Modern Irrigation Management
- Ornament Gardening and Landscaping
- Medicinal Plants
- Flower Cultivation
- Vegetable Seed Production
- Small Millets Cultivation and Value Addition
- Cotton and Maize Hybrid Seed Production
- Waste Land Development

Central University, Hyderabad

Centre for Distance and Virtual Learning of Central University Hyderabad offers the following Postgraduate Diploma Programmes:

1. P.G. Diploma in Project Management
2. P.G. Diploma in Business Management
3. P.G. Diploma in Library Automation and Networking
4. P.G. Diploma in Chemical Analysis and Quality Management
5. P.G. Diploma in Cyber Laws andIntellectual Property Rights
6. P.G. Diploma in Communicative English
7. P.G. Diploma in Criminal Justice and Forensic Science
8. P.G. Diploma in Telecommunication
9. P.G. Diploma in Governance

10. P.G. Diploma in Medicinal Botany
11. P.G. Diploma in Human Rights
12. P.G. Diploma in Translation Studies in Hindi

Technical Programmes through Distance and Mixed Mode

Technical programmes through distance mode were initiated first by Birla Institute of Technology and Science, Pilani (1979) and Jawaharlal Nehru Technology University, Hyderabad (1983) as continuing and distance education programmes and collaborative work integrated learning for in-service Diploma holders. Subsequently, IGNOU started Advanced Diploma programmes in Water Resource Engineering and Construction Management (1996), which were subsequently upgraded to bachelor level programmes (2006). YCMOU, Nashik (1996) and Karnataka State Open University also launched technical programmes. Around the year 2000 several conventional and Deemed Universities, to name a few, JRN Rajasthan Vidyapeeth deemed University, Udaipur; IASE Deemed, University, Sardarshahr, Rajasthan; Vinayaka Missions Deemed University, Salem, Tamil Nadu and Allahabad Agriculture Institute Deemed University, Allahabad, Uttar Pradesh now renamed as Sam Higginbottom Institute of Agriculture, Technology and Sciences, Allahabad started offering technical programmes in Engineering through distance mode.

Engineering Programmes

Some details about the institutions offering engineering programmes are provided as under:

Jawaharlal Nehru Technological University, Hyderabad

Jawaharlal Nehru Technological University, Hyderabad has introduced the correspondence-cum-contact programme in different specialisations (Civil Engineering, Mechanical Engineering, Electrical and Electronics Engineering, Electronics and Communication Engineering) from the academic year 1983 onwards and the specialisation in Computer Science and Engineering from 1999 onwards.

Duration and Eligibility: The duration of these programmes is four years. Admission is Open to Diploma holders in concerned branch of Engineering with one year experience and working in the State of Andhra Pradesh at the time of the application.

Credit System: The B.Tech programme is offered on the basis of credit system to have flexibility in the system. A student can have the choice in courses of study and go through the programme at his own pace. Unit system is adopted, giving eight credits for the theory and four credits for Lab courses. Each course is treated as independent unit for evaluation and successful completion.

Instructional Material: Printed instructional material is made available for home study. The syllabus is broken into units. Lab manuals are supplied for each lab course. Assignments are appended for students' response besides self assessment questions at the end of each unit. The assignments are evaluated and returned to the candidates pointing out the inadequacies in the responses.

Personal Contact programmes are arranged for theory and practicals for 2-3 weeks continuously and conducted at Anantapur, Kakinada and Hyderabad centres. While the attendance in theory contact programme is optional, attendance in practicals is compulsory.

Birla Institute of Technology and Science Pilani

Birla Institute of Technology and Sciences (BITS), Pilani is a deemed University established in 1964. The institute has been participating in the human resource development activities of the industries by evolving several degree diploma programmes which integrate the working environment of the employees with the learning environment required by the Institute. Such programmes were initiated in the year 1979 at the request of the industries hosting Practice School Programmes. M.E. (Collaborative) programme in Project Engineering was started in association with Development Consultants (P) Ltd., Kolkata and in Industrial Production in association with GRASIM, Nagda.

The education in work-integrated learning programmes of BITS is characterised by person-centered approach with the rigour and standards at par with Institute's on-campus system of education. These programmes combine the flexibility and ingenuity of the off-campus educational system with the regular features of the on-campus education system. Also, the learning and evaluation process draws upon the successful and established methodologies followed by the Institute. All the programmes follow a semester and a credit based system.

Thapar University, Patiala, Punjab

Thapar University is delivering engineering education since 1956 through conventional mode and is considered one of the prestigious institutes in India in engineering and technology. The University has also started Distance Education Programme in Engineering which is open for practising professionals who hold a diploma in engineering and are employed. This provides an opportunity to these working professionals to renew their knowledge. The University admits a very small fraction of the working professionals in these programmes through competitive tests. Number of admission is restricted around 200 in each session. To ensure quality study material the University has published about 90 Self Instruction Materials written by their faculty and reviewed by faculty of HTS. The interactive lectures are delivered online through dedicated internet servers. The evaluation is spread over the entire semester through assignments, quizes and end-semester examinations. The students carry out an industry project in the final semester in collaboration with their employers. The programme is considered rigorous and meticulous in admission, delivery and evaluation.

Indira Gandhi National Open University, New Delhi

The School of Engineering and Technology of the IGNOU has the responsibility of initiating academic, continuing and extension education programmes in the areas of engineering and technology. Since 1995 the School has developed several programmes aimed at increasing job potential and economic advantage to the learners. To fulfill its mandate, the School regularly interacts with employing agencies, professional bodies and industry so as to reflect educational and training needs of the targeted learners in the curriculum. The school practises participative and collaborative strategy by inviting different industries. The Self Instructional Materials are designed and developed with the help of experts drawn from various institutions of acknowledged expertise: IITs, National Institutes of Technology (NITs), reputed Universities and Engineering Colleges and Industry.

The University offers both short-term and long-term programmes leading to Certificates, Diplomas or Degrees, covering conventional as well as innovative programmes. Most of these programmes have been developed after an initial survey of the demand for such studies. They are launched with a view to fulfill the student's need for certification, improvement of skills, acquisition of professional qualification, continuing education and professional development at work place, self-enrichment, and diversification of knowledge.

The School has the following programmes:

- Bachelor of Technology in Construction Management, Water Resources Engineering and Mechanical Engineering (Computer Integrated Manufacturing)
- Bachelor of Technology, Advanced Diploma in Construction Management (ADCM)
- Advance Diploma in Water Resources Engineering (ADWRE)
- Advanced Diploma in Computer Integrated Manufacturing (ADCIM)
- Diploma in Civil Engineering (Army Personnel (DCLE)

- Diploma in Civil Engineering (General Candidates) (DCLE-G)
- Diploma in Mechanical Engineering (DME)

Yashwantrao Chavan Maharashtra Open University, Nashik

The YCMOU, Nashik, Maharashtra started offering technical programmes in Engineering w.e.f. 1996 when it launched Diploma level programmes in the areas of Communication Engineering, Computer Technology, Industrial Electronics and Instrumentation Engineering. In the year 2004 the YCMOU further launched four Diploma level programmes in the areas of Mechanical, Production, Automobile and Thermal Engineering. It also launched B. Tech programmes in the Marine, Electronics and Mechanical engineering in 2004. The dissemination of education is through blended mode. Support system includes web based discussion forums. Cost-effectiveness of programmes is an added advantage. The intake of students in both the semesters of a year is approximately 10,000.

Karnataka State Open University, Mysore

The University offers technical programmes like Diploma in Engineering, B.Tech and M.Tech. For this purpose KSOU collaborates with institutions to conduct classes in the institutions/colleges recognised by AICTE and other bodies. Details regarding the programmes are not made available.

Offer of Technical Programmes by Technical Universities and Deemed Universities

There was sudden increase in the number of technical programmes after the year 2000 as a few Private and deemed Universities such as JRN Rajasthan Vidyapeeth deemed University, Udaipur; IASE Deemed University, Sardarshahr, Rajasthan and Allahabad Agriculture Institute now renamed as Sam Higginbottom Institute of Agriculture, Technology and Sciences, Allahabad — started offering programmes such as Diploma in Engineering, B.Tech and M.Tech programmes. Many more Universities and Institutions have followed the suit. Some of them have even franchised the programme delivery and even established study centres in non-AICTE approved Colleges. This subsequently became an issue for ensuring quality in technical/ professional programmes. Because of the high demand of technical and managerial expertise and the value of such degrees, the ODL mode has emerged as offering solution but in the process it has dented its credibility so much that employers have started ignoring their degrees/ certificates.

Management Education

National Policy on Education, (1986) on Technical and Management Education

The National Policy on Education (NPE), 1986 provides that "Although the two streams of technical and management education are functioning separately, it is essential to look at them together, in view of their close relationship and complementary concerns. The reorganisation of Technical and Management Education should take into account the anticipated scenario by the turn of the century, with specific reference to the likely changes in the economy, social environment, production and management processes, the rapid expansion of knowledge and the great advances in science and technology".

As per the NPE, "the infrastructure and services sectors as well as the unorganised rural sector also need a greater induction of improved technologies and a supply of technical and managerial manpower."

The NPE further lays emphasis on promotion of continuing education, covering established as well as emerging technologies.

The NPE (1986) also states that "as computers have become important and ubiquitous tools, a minimal exposure to computers and training in their use will form a part of professional education. Programmes of computer literacy will be organised on wide scale from the school stage".

It has put special emphasis on offering of technical and management programmes through distance mode. The NPE states that "In View of the present rigid entry requirements to formal courses restricting the access of a large segment of people to technical and managerial education, programmes through a distance-learning process, including use of the mass media will be offered. Technical and management education programmes, including education in polytechnics, will also be on a flexible modular pattern based on credits, with provision for multi-point entry. A strong guidance and counselling service will be provided".

It further elaborates that "appropriate formal and non-formal programmes of technical education will be devised for the benefit of women, the economically and socially weaker sections, and the physically handicapped. The emphasis of vocational education and its expansion will need a large number of teachers and professionals in vocational education, educational technology, curriculum development, etc. Programmes will be started to meet this demand. To encourage students to consider "self-employment" as a career option, training in entrepreneurship will be provided through modular or optional courses, in degree or diploma programmes. In order to meet the continuing needs of updating curriculum, renewal should systematically phase out obsolescence and introduce new technologies of disciplines".

As per the NPE, the All India Council for Technical Education, which has been given statutory status, will be responsible for planning, formulation and the maintenance of norms and standards, accreditation, funding of priority areas, monitoring and evaluation, maintaining parity of certification and awards and ensuring the co-ordinated and integrated development of technical and management education. Mandatory periodic evaluation will be carried out by a duly constituted Accreditation Board. The Council will be strengthened and it will function in a decentralised manner with greater involvement of State governments and technical institutions of good quality. In the interests of maintaining standards and for several other valid reasons, the commercialisation of technical and professional education will be curbed. An alternative system will be devised to involve private and voluntary effort in this sector of education, in conformity with accepted norms and goals.

However, the AICTE, as a policy, does not recognise technical education through ODL mode except MBA and MCA. As a result, the AICTE has not felt the need to develop benchmarks for offering other technical and management programmes through distance mode. In fact, the AICTE policy to allow only MBA and MCA programmes through ODL mode does not seem to be in consonance with the NPE, 1986.

Need for Alternative System:

Globalisation and the advent of communication and information technologies have opened up many new possibilities for training and re-training of personnel working in industry. Many of the multinational companies want upgradation of knowledge and skills of staff at work place. Distance mode has the potential to impart work integrated learning without disturbing normal schedule of work at the places of employment. Further, there are large number of employees, Diploma holders working in Government Departments, PSUs and other organisations and there is very little scope for such employees for vertical mobility. Distance mode can be used effectively to upgrade knowledge and skill of such experienced employees to graduate level and thus allow for their vertical mobility.

Use of only one media may not be adequate for delivery of technical programmes. Three basic requirements for technical programmes delivery are — organisation of (a) theory courses, (b) interaction, and (c) practical components. These three components can be incorporated in the programme by using SLM in hard as well as soft forms for theory component, face-to-face/ e-learning for interaction and compulsory practical component for development of requisite skill. Practice at will can also be facilitated through simulations. E-learning provides all essential core teaching-learning components like interaction, evaluation and feedback. Regular face-to-face contact in form of counselling sessions during weekends or during off-time of colleges should be used for clarification and removal of doubts of learners. Laboratory experiments could be conducted in AICTE recognised colleges taking into account the physical infrastructure and human resource required for the purpose.

Conventional universities running such programmes are also making use of lectures and chunks of learning materials through ICT as a supplementary teaching/ learning method. NPTEL and NMEICT are engaged in the development of such e-resources. Such quality course material through national expertise can easily be adopted by the Technical Education Providers. As conventional system is getting strengthened through technology enabled distance mode lectures and tutorials, it is only logical to expect that ICT enabled delivery in ODL system combined with face to face, counselling, tutorials and laboratory works will ensure quality in ODL system also.

Therefore, the mode of teaching/ learning for the contemporary era cannot be exclusively in conventional or in distance education mode. It has to be a proper mix of the two which can be termed as blended learning. Having regard to the advent of ICT, developments taking place all around the world including in India and the vision enshrined in the National Policy of Education, 1986, a fresh look needs to be taken by the AICTE on offering Technical and Management Programmes through ODL mode.

6

Student Enrolment and Dropout

Distance Students are heterogeneous. The common demographic characteristics of distance students are:

- Of all castes and communities
- Of all ages
- Of both genders
- Mostly from urban areas
- Socially disadvantaged
- Predominantly working adults with multiple roles in society
- Studying part time
- With diversified life and educational background.

Normally, the following persons join distance education institutions.

- school leavers who are qualified for traditional university entry but cannot be admitted because of non-availability of places in traditional universities and colleges.
- adults who desire to acquire university level qualifications but cannot choose not to apply for entry to a traditional university because they
    a) lack education qualifications required for entry.
    b) have family commitments, especially to young children, which tie them to their homes.
    c) prefer to study independently
    d) live in institutions (e.g. the handicapped) which they are unable to leave.
    e) are in full-time employments and cannot or choose not to give up their jobs.
- teachers professional and manpower groups who require vocational training, professional updating and increased knowledge levels but cannot be released from their employments to attend a campus based university or training college.
- adults who wish to pursue lifelong learning opportunities (continuing education) unrelated to the pursuit of a degree level qualification.

Advantages of Distance Learners

- highly motivated
- goal oriented
- highly focussed

- rich in life experience
- with more qualifications
- self-aware
- with good memories of schooling
- concerned with getting value from time and money.

Disadvantages of Distance Learners

- with little preparation.
- with very rusty study experience.
- haunted by negative memories of schooling.
- forced to study in a less favourable environment.
- low level of support.
- lack of any immediate feedback.
- lack of study time.
- short intermitted study periods.

Enrolment in Higher Education: Conventional System and Open Universities System

	In Conventional System	*In Open Universities*	*Show of Total Enrolment to Higher Education*
1993-94	5817249	170372	2.85%
2003-04	10201981	75032	6.97%
2010-11	18670050	1916247	10.26%
2013-14	23765000	2104291	8.86%

Profile of Distance Learners in State Open Universities

Year	*Female*	*Rural*	*SC*	*ST*	*OBC*
2003-04	35.1	49.3	13.9	4.6	38.6
2009-10	39.8	53.7	13.4	6.5	30.0
2013-14	41.9	53.4	15.8	9.1	34.1

Distance Education in India

Year	*No. of Institutes*	*Students in millions*
1981	22	0.17
1990-91	40	0.59
2000-01	74	1.38
2007-08	144	2.74
2011-12	197	4.20

Enrolment of Students at IGNOU

1999 – 172550
2000 – 196650
2001 – 291360
2002 – 301724
2003 – 316547
2004 – 334415
2005 – 366161
2006 – 429542
2007 – 468444
2008 – 550600
2009 – 555310
2014 – 722390
2017 – 821658

Enrolment in Open Universities in India

1983 – 84	6231
1987 – 88	47670
1990 – 91	102820
1996 – 97	316580
2000 – 01	623892
2006 – 07	1120561
2011 – 12	2114510
2013 – 14	2104291

Enrolment in Conventional and Open Universities Systems in India

Year	*Enrolment in Conventional System*	*Enrolment in Open University System*
1983-84	3307649	6231
1990-91	4924868	102820
1995-96	6574005	256742
2003-04	10201981	750342
2013-14	23765000	2104291

Level wise Distribution of Distance Education Students Enrolment in India

Programme	*Males*	*Females*	*Total*
Ph.D.	87	49	136
PG	510526	597836	1108362
UG	1421708	1077682	2499390

PG Diploma	41383	27252	68635
Diploma	64175	40053	104228
Certificates	17374	26775	44149
Integrated	1	0	1
All	2055254	1769647	3824901

Why drop out?

In trying to understand why some students succeed while others drop out? We must understand the complex inter play of certain "Push" and "Pull" factors. "Push" factors encourage them to continue while "Pull" factors lead to withdrawl. A simplified picture of the "Pull" and "Push" factors acting on an imaginary individual is:

"Push" Factors

- Wants degree to get promotion
- Likes to finish something started
- Very interested in the subject matter
- Spouse is very encouraging
- Allowed time for summer school.

"Pull" Factors

- Want to spend time with family
- Courses are very difficult
- Fees are high
- Does not like tutor
- Part time degree course available nearby.

Each of these factors will have different strengths and drop out will occur when the "Pull" factors barely outweigh the "Push" factors. Some students begin their course with "Pull" factors and they are very vulnerable. In other cases the "Push" factors greatly exceed the "Pull" ones.

The authors of a research study of BRAOU and IGNOU students identified the types of students dropping out tendencies.

- Very old and very young students are more likely to drop out.
- Men are more in danger of dropping out than women.
- Dropping out is greater when the level of previous schooling is lower.
- Student of Science and Technology are more in danger of dropping out than students of Arts.
- More courses the students enrolled for, the higher the dropout rate.

- Among students who regularly attend activities at study centres, the dropout rate is low.
- Student who get counselling services from the institutions regularly, drop out is low among them.

Research studies on certain Indian State Open Universities students in Northern India listed several factors which can underlie drop out from student's perspective. Some of such factors are:

- Course factors
- Institutional factors
- Study environment factors
- Personal blame
- Motivational factors

7

Instructional System

A distinguishing feature of a distance education system is its multi-media instructional system. Multi-media instructional system is learner based, while the instructional system of a conventional system is teacher based. In this system teachers are absent and learners are independent and mostly learn for themselves with the help of multi-media instructional packages. It is said that in a distance system the institution teaches whereas in a conventional system the teacher teaches.

Broadly the instructional method of a distance education system consists of the following:

1. Print

- Self-Instructional texts or lessons
- Set texts
- Supplementary materials

2. Broadcast Audio-visual

- Radio
- TV

3. Non-broadcast Audio-visual

- Audio-cassettes
- Video tapes
- Discs
- Filmstrips/ slides
- Films/ Film-loops
- Computer systems

4. Practical/ Project Work

- Home kits
- Laboratory experience
- Field work
- Computing

5. Inter-personal Communication

- Correspondence tuition
- Telephone contact

- Tutorial classes
- Counselling sessions
- Self-help groups
- Residential schools

A developed distance education institution's instructional system comprises:

- Textbooks specially designed and printed for OU courses.
- Supplementary readings of various types.
- Regular computer-marked and tutor-marked assignments and final examinations.
- Television and radio broadcasts.
- Teaching aids of many types including audiocassettes, games and laboratory kits.
- Centralised and regionalised library resources.
- Organised tutorial sessions.
- Regional study centres.
- Organised study groups.
- Tutoring by telephone.
- Guidance and counselling services, particularly in self-study methods.
- Field trips, workshops, laboratory sessions.

IGNOU

The University follows a multimedia approach for instruction, which comprises:

a) Self Instructional Written Material: The printed study material (written in self-instructional style) for both theory and practical components of the programmes is supplied to the learners in batches of blocks for every course (on an average one block per credit). A block which comes in the form of a booklet usually comprises 3 to 5 units.

b) Audio-visual Material Aids: The learning package contains audio and video CDs which have been produced by the University for better clarification and enhancement of understanding of the course material given to the learners. A video programme is normally of 25-30 minutes duration. The video cassettes are screened at the study centres during specific sessions which are duly notified for the benefit of the learners. The video programmes are telecast on National Network of Doordarshan and Gyan Darshan. All Gyan Vani stations are broadcasting curriculum based audio programmes. In addition, some selected stations of All India Radio are also broadcasting the audio programmes. Learners can confirm the dates for the programmes from their study centres. The information is also provided through the university website.

c) Counselling Sessions: Normally counselling sessions are held as per schedule drawn up by the study centres. These are mostly held outside the regular working hours of the host institutions where the study centres are located.

d) Teleconferences: Live teleconferencing sessions are conducted via satellite through interactive Gyan Darshan Channel as well as simulcasted on Edusat channel from the University studios at EMPC, the schedule of which is made available at the study centres.

e) Practicals/ Project Work: Some Programmes have practical/ project component also. Practicals are held at designated institutions for which schedule is provided by the study centres. Attendance at practicals is compulsory. For project work, comprehensive project guide, in the form of a booklet, is provided to the students along with the study materials.

BRAOU

The Expert Committee on the Establishment of BRAOU strongly suggested the use of multi media for instructional purpose. The Expert Committee recommended TV and Radio broadcasts as well as audio-video programmes to be used as an integral part of the instruction to enrich support, illuminate, demonstrate or otherwise strengthen the learning experiences of courses.

Following the Expert Committee Report the University designed and evolved a multi media instructional system comprising:

- course units — specially structured course books which form the core of the teaching material.
- radio programmes — these are normally relatively less important supplement to the course units, although they form the part of the university's teaching which is well known to the public at large.
- programmes on audiotapes — these are either broadcast on AIR or independently produced for presentation at study centres.
- programmes on videotapes — these are specially developed for presentation at the study centres for students and academic counsellors and coordinators.

- face-to-face tutorial sessions at study centres.
- counselling services to students by the coordinators, academic counsellors and the academic heads of host institutions at study centres.
- summer schools and intensive counselling programmes.
- project works.
- practical experiences for science courses at select study centres.

Instructional System of BRAOU

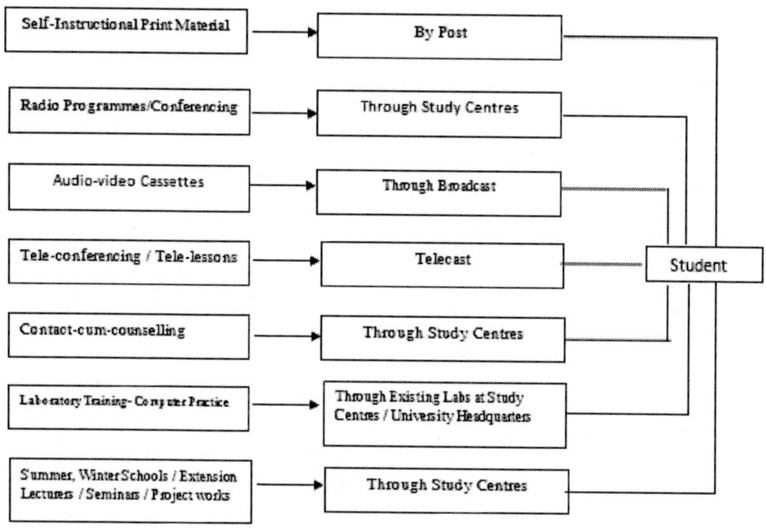

Tamil Nadu Open University

The University follows a multi-media approach for the instruction of students consisting of the followings.

1. Self Instructional Material
2. Counseling Sessions
3. Practicals/ Project Works
4. Gyan Darshan Educational Channel
5. Gyan Vani
6. Interactive Radio Counselling

8

Student Assignments

An unhappy feature of Indian distance education institutions is that many of them do not have student assignment system. Most of the Correspondence Courses Institutes of conventional universities (dual mode universities) lack the component of student assignment. The first Open University in India (BRAOU0 too does not have the proper system of student assignments. With the establishment of IGNOU in 1985, the significance of student assignment has been realised by many distance teaching universities. As is found by research studies one of the main reasons for student drop out in distance education is the lack of assignments component in distance education institutions. Importance, purposes, types and student's perspective of assignments are briefly described below.

Assignments enable students to test how effectively they have been studying their courses. Through them students receive evidence about their own progress and guidance to improve it. They constitute a dynamic tool for a dialogue between the teacher and the students. They invite active and meaningful participation of the student and provide a tool for monitoring progress and assessing achievement. Assignments for submission give learners an opportunity to converse with the tutor, to receive advice on their problems and to confirm their understanding of the problem. Through the assessed assignments the distance teacher is able to check the student's progress and assess their strengths and weaknesses. In a way they compel students to read the materials and therefore promote active learning beyond the passive reading of the course material. The importance of assignments as an integral part of distance teaching-learning is evidenced by the fact that they constitute up to considerable percentage of the final grade in courses of many distanced education institution. They constitute up to 50per cent final score of courses in the British Open University and up to 30 per cent in Indira GandhiNational Open University.

Functions and Purposes of Assignment

Assignments, as mentioned above, serve a variety of functions. According to surveys conducted by several DE institutions, they

- give students effective feedback through which students correct their mistakes and control their progress.
- motivate the students.

- enable teachers to evaluate student's achievements during the course, so that they can give each student help.
- provide the opportunity for tutors to motivate students by giving them encouragement and praise.
- activate the students.
- give students opportunities for application and transfer of their knowledge.
- focus the student's attention on important learning objectives.
- develop the methods of retraining knowledge and the practice.
- enable students to revise the whole study units.
- provide opportunities for students to develop skills in survey, summing up and integrating various parts of units.
- compel students to develop regularity of work.
- create opportunities for contacts between teachers and students thereby counteracting student's feeling of isolation assignments, according to Phil Race, serve several useful purposes.
- help learners prepare for formal exams (where relevant).
- give learners feedback comments on their work, and develop their self-confidence.
- give learners a measure of how successful (or otherwise) their work is.
- form basis for communication between learners and their tutors.
- provide learners with deadlines and stages to help them structure the timing of their work
- maintain and develop learners' motivation and commitment to their studies.

Types of Assignments

Assignments are broadly of two types:

- Tutor Marked Assignments (TMAs)
- Computer Marked Assignments (CMAs)

TMA has several forms:

- Open and Unstructured Essay
- Structured Essay
- Role Play Essay
- Interpretation of Data
- Design
- Project
- Description of process
- Notes
- Definition

- Hypothesis
- Calculation
- Sketch
- Critical Review.

Ways in which Tutors Teach through their Written Comments on Assignments

In many ways written comments are used by tutors. They

- draw the learners' attention to facts they have overlooked or misinterpreted.
- suggest alternative explanations or interpretations.
- guide learners on the handling of evidence.
- show how to use quotations from texts.
- draw attention to gaps in the learners' reasoning.
- suggest how learners might present their ideas more effectively.
- offer new data that will help learners extend their understanding.
- ask for further explanation of muddled answers.
- demonstrate short-cuts in problem-solving.
- draw attention to how a piece of work might have been improved, e.g. in content, balance or logic.
- point out relationships between the learner's present work and their earlier work.
- commend the learners for any unexpected insights, special efforts or improvement in skills.

Types of Tutor Comments

Comments of a distance teacher on the assignment responses of a learner help the learners: (a) to sustain interest in learning, (b) to get motivated and activated, (c) to facilitate learning, and (d) to assess his progress in comparison with others. Tutor comments, therefore, should be necessarily of teaching type. If they are not of teaching type, they defeat the purpose of teaching-learning at a distance.

Tutor comments can be broadly classified into two kinds:

Non-Teaching Comments	**Teaching Comments**
- Harmful comments	- Positive comments
- Hollow comments	- Constructive comments
- Misleading comments	- Global comments
- Null comments	- Personal comments
- Negative comments	

Students' Perspective of Tutor's Comments

A research study highlighted that what students want from tutor's comments. The following are desired by distance learners:

- to have their work treated with respect from an instructional point of view, to get the grades necessary to pass the course.
- fair and objective grading.
- an explanation and justification of the grade.
- to know the significance of the grade (e.g. that 'C' is a good solid grade) and when letter grades are used, to know where they come within the grade and if there has been an improvement even if the grade is the same.
- a clear indication of now they can improve both in terms of the specific question and more generally. This is particularly important to students who feel stuck in a grade.
- a sympathetic, friendly and supportive approach, indicating that the tutor is 'on their side'.
- not to be talked down to or patronised.
- encouragement and reassurance about their own ability, but balanced with honesty.
- positive comments and not simply negative, critical ones.
- specific comments (e.g. indicating clearly the strengths and weaknesses of the assignment, giving useful references) not vague generalities.
- constructive criticism and advice (e.g. not simply to be told that they have gone wrong but in what way, and what to do about it to indicate references to the course material to indicate where to find what they have missed/ misunderstood, etc.).
- full comments (in particular on the script itself), since these can be of value not only at that time but for revision purposes in the case of the stronger student, to be challenged.

9

Self Instructional Material

Self Instructional Materials (SIM) are the main basis for distance teaching-learning. Teaching through SIM has been fast growing both in developed and developing countries. SIM in print is the dominant medium for distance teaching in all distance education institutions.

In a conventional classroom the teacher transmits the content of the course and helps the students to absorb and use the contents. The teacher also helps students learn. In many ways the teacher helps student learning.

In distance education system students are away from the teachers. The teacher's role is performed by SIM. The various forms of support provided in classroom interaction are built into the SIM themselves. SIM thus become sources both of content and support.

SIM differ from textbooks and journal articles which are organised in terms of the subject matter rather than as aids to learning.

SIM are totally different from normal textbook used by on-campus students. The difference between textbook and SIM is briefly summarised by Roger Lewis and Nigel Paine as shown below.

Difference between Textbooks and Self Instructional Material (SIM)

Textbooks	*SIM*
Assume interest	Arouse interest
Written for teacher's use also	Written for learner use
Designed for a wide market	Designed for identified groups
Rarely give objectives	Always give objectives
One route through	Many routes through
Structured according to logic of the content	Structured according to needs of learner
Little or no self-assessment	Major emphasis on self-assessment
Ignore likely learner difficulties	Address learner difficulties
Rarely offer summaries	Always offer summaries
Impersonal style	Personal style
Dense in content	Content unpacked

Densely packed appearance	Well-spaced-out appearance
Packaged for sale	Packaged for use
No mechanism to collect learner views	Learners' evaluation sought
No study skills advice	Provide study skills advice

Self Instructional Material

- self-explanatory
- self-contained
- self-directed
- self-motivating
- self-evaluating
- self-learning

Functions of SIM

- Help the individual learners find their way into and around the subject by repeating the content.
- Tell them what they need to do before tackling the material.
- Make clear what they should be able to do on the completion of the material.
- Advise them how to tackle the work.
- Explain the subject matter in such a way that the learners can relate it to what they already know.
- Encourage them sufficiently to make whatever effort is needed in coming to grips with the subject.
- Engage them in exercises and activities that make them work with the subject matter rather than merely read about it.
- Give the learners feedback on these exercises and activities enabling them to judge for themselves whether they are learning successfully.
- Help them to sum up their learning at the end of the unit.

The chief characteristic of SIM is known as learning activeness. Materials are learner active, if they have the potential to interest learners to work and be involved in different types of academic activities such as noting the points, absorbing the concepts, collecting allied material applying what has been learnt to a new situation, doing self-check exercises, writing assignment responses and similar activities. Such built-in strategies make material learner active and pedagogically meaningful.

Access devices are those devices which help the course writers go on to their learners as closely as they can, and help the learners come as close to the content as they can. These devices also help the learners find their way into the text. There are three main functions of these access devices.

- They enable learners to find what they need to read in the unit, i.e., the means and ways to reach the content.
- They make the content more intimate to learners and help them grasp what is presented in the unit.
- They perform the functions of a live classroom teacher i.e., build a teacher in the text.

Some of the access devices are:

- Title
- Structure of the Unit
- Objectives
- Division of content
- Illustrations
- Glossaries
- Instructions.

Many distance education institutions in India, particularly dual mode universities, do not provide self-instructional materials for their learners. They do not invest on the preparation of SIM. They persue either standard textbooks and/ or prepare instructional materials in the traditional textbook fashion. Since the advent of IGNOU in 1985, STRIDE of IGNOU provides training to the academics in dual mode university on the development and revision of self-learning materials. STRIDE produced a Handbook dealing extensively on the process of development of self-learning materials and revision of the materials. This Handbook is meant for those who are working or intend to work distance education system, and also for those who want to know how to develop self-learning materials for distance learners and how to revise those materials periodically.

It is high time that dual mode institutions and private organisations providing distance education get benefited by IGNOU efforts and make learning materials really self-instructional.

10
Use of Technology

There has been rapid expansion of technologies available for education and many countries are able to use these for their educational purposes. The factors that influence the fast growth of technologies include:

- the capacity, competence, flexibility and appropriateness of technologies are rapidly increasing,
- conventional educational systems and models are slowly becoming inappropriate to meet the new challenges resulting from the explosion of new knowledge,
- the need for continuing education is growing — a trend that will be compounded as the population base increases,
- increasing desire for lifelong learning opportunities at places and paces convenient to people,
- the belief and realisation that quality of learning can be greatly enhanced by the application of new technologies,
- the demand for remote and distance learners for equitable access to learning opportunities,
- in an increasingly globalised society, opportunities and occasions are emerging to work collaboratively with colleagues across the world, and
- the ability to partner with other educational institutions provides benefits economically and educationally.

We are now witnessing a major restructuring of our social, industrial and educational institutions and an increased reliance on technologies for work and education in general and distance education in particular.

Since the advent of the Open University System, developments in technology have led to four major trends:

- a wider range of media is now available for use in the home;
- there is a greater diversity of access to new media;
- the costs are coming down for new media; and
- new media are giving students greater control over their learning and greater interaction.

Various technologies now available for distance education are:

- Audio cassettes
- Audio conferencing
- Cable TV
- Computer based audio-graphics systems
- Computer-based learning
- Computer-based multimedia
- Computer controlled interactive video
- Computer conferencing
- Digital video discs
- Electronic mail
- E-portfolios
- Internet
- Laser video discs
- Mobile phones
- Portals
- Remote interactive data bases
- Satellite TV
- Search engines
- Simulations
- Telephone teaching
- Teletext
- Viewdata
- Video discs
- Video conferencing

Technologies used in distance education can be classified into three main groups, i.e. audio technologies, video technologies and computer-based technologies. A further distinction is the mode of utilisation, which can be either one-way (non-interactive mode) or two-way (interactive mode). These technologies are often combined in various configurations, thus multiplying their modes of application and increasing flexibility of their utilisation.

Non-interactive and Interactive Technologies

Technology	Non-interactive	Interactive
Audio	Radio (primary carrier) Radio (subcarrier) Audio tape	Telephone Audio teleconferencing

Video	Open-broadcasting television Cable television (one-way) Videotape Instructional Television Fixed Service (ITFS) Satellite television (one-way) Slow Scam/ Freeze frame television (one-way)	Microwave (point-to-point) Cable television (two-way or Viewer-response) Slow scan/ freeze frame television (two-way) Electronic blackboard Satellite television (two-way) Video teleconferencing
Computer		Computer-Assisted Instruction Computer-Based Instructional Management

Selection of Valid Mix of Technologies

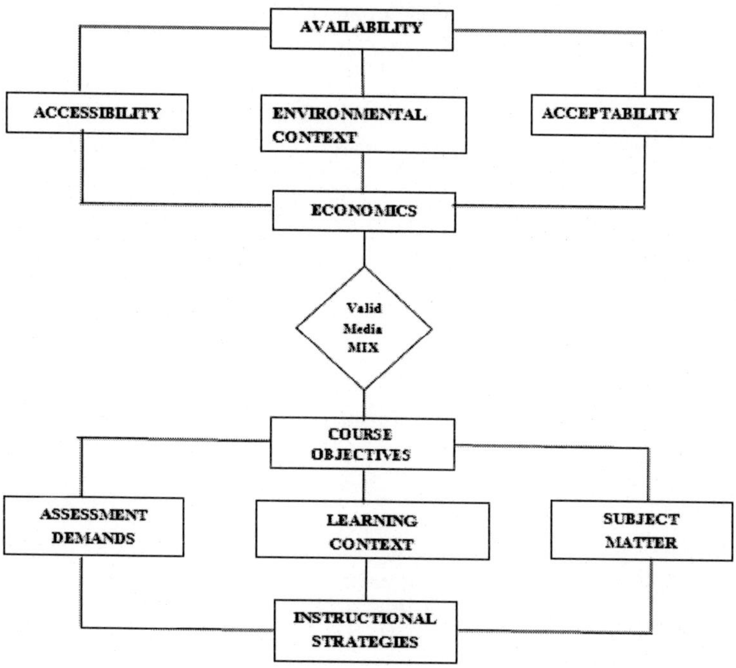

IGNOU

The decision to use technology, other than print, was intended to enhance the effectiveness of teaching-learning and for reaching a wider group of learners in remote rural, tribal and isolated areas.

Audio and Video: Audio and Video cassette based programmes have been produced since 1987 by the erstwhile Communication Division, to largely play a supplementary role to the SIM. The Communication Division was upgraded into EMPC in 1996.

Radio and Television: Television broadcasting started in 1991 throughout the national network of Doordarshan on three days in a week, subsequently increased to five days a week.

EMPC has a wide range of media production facilities.

Teleconferencing: IGNOU conducted the first 10 day teleconferencing experiment in 1993 through extended C-Band and satellite uplink support provided by ISRO. The Teleconferencing system connected IGNOU, IGNOU Regional Centres and State Open Universities. The experiment of 1993 led to its regular use by IGNOU and other organisations for education and training.

Interactive Radio Counselling: IGNOU got into IRC in 1998 as an experimental programme for one year conducted at Bhopal AIR. In 1999 IRC was extended to eight other IRCS.

Today many radio stations broadcast programmes for one hour every Sunday.

Gyan Darshan: This is a full dedicated educational channel in the country for educational and development programming. This was launched jointly by HRD Ministry, Prasar Bharati and IGNOU. Educational programmes for GD are contributed by IGNOU, UGC-CEC, NCERT-CIET, NIOS and some governmental and non-educational organisations.

Gyan Vani: A shift from IRC is Gyan Vani, a Radio Cooperative devoted exclusively for education and development, created by MHRD, Government of India.

The academic aspects of educational media development and use of IGNOU are detailed in *Stride Hand Book on Media and Technology in DE.*

BRAOU

A unique feature of BRAOU is its wide use of technology in distance teaching. Conventional universities and their correspondence institutes in the State do not use any modern technology in teaching. BRAOU has been using, radio, television, audio cassettes, video cassettes, teleconferencing for instructional purposes. The books *India's First Open University: Two Decades Journey* by C. Sesharatnam and *India's First Open University: Experiences of Two Decades* by V.S. Prasad and V.Venkaiah give detailed picture of technology use in BRAOU.

Some academics in distance teaching institutions in Andhra Pradesh conducted research studies on the use of technology in single mode and dual mode distance teaching universities in the State. Researchers found that many distance learners do not make use of media facilities provided by the University. Students' opinions and experiences in this regard are significant. The main reasons expressed by the academic staff at the headquarters and study centers as well as students are the following:

Non-utilisation of Electronic Media

On the issue of non-utilisation at electronic media by students experiences and opinions are collected by the researchers from a sample of students, academic staff members, academic counsellors and study centre Heads. Students gave 10 reasons; academic staff members gave 14 reasons and academic counsellors gave seven reasons. Study centre Heads gave reasons similar to those of counsellors. The significant common reasons indicated by all the four categories are the following:

1. Printed course materials supplied by the University are self-sufficient and self-directing for student study.
2. Contents of electronic media programmes are already in the printed course materials.
3. Electronic media programmes are not made compulsory for students by the University. Examinations do not include questions on media programmes.
4. Media programmes cover very few aspects of very few course subjects.
5. Students of regular colleges and universities do not use electronic media. Then why for distance students?
6. Media programme schedules are not available in advance to students.
7. Counselling sessions are held at study centres on Sundays. Some media programmes are also on Sundays. Due to the clash, students cannot use media programmes.
8. Most of the academic counsellors and study centre Heads do not take interest in motivating students towards the use of non-print media.
9. Many First year UG students develop drop out tendency and are not bothered about print and non-print media.
10. Broadcast/ telecast timings are not suitable to students.
11. Most of the study centres do not have proper equipment and facilities for presentation of audio and video programmes on cassettes.
12. MANA TV reception facilities are very limited in view of their technical non-availability.
13. Most of the students do not have educational media habit.

14. Most of the non-print media programmes are simple lectures and lack visuals and hence do not create appeal.
15. All radio and television broadcasts are not available at study centres on cassettes and tapes. Hence, even a small number of interested students cannot have access to media programmes.

Suggestions for Effective and Efficient Use of Technology

While assessing the role of technology in its academic and administrative operations, the University should consider the various suggestions made by academic staff, academic counsellors and study centre Heads. Common suggestions of significance and relevance offered by the key managers of the University are following:

1. Induction meetings for newly admitted students every year should be held at study centres for orienting students on the usefulness of technology for student learning.
2. Student Handbooks for all courses should include advantages of print and non-print technologies to students in their learning.
3. Academic counsellors and study centre Heads should motivate the students towards the use of non-print electronic media programmes.
4. All radio broadcasts and television broadcasts of the University should be put on cassettes/ tapes/ CDs/ DVDs, and be made available to students at study centres.
5. Maximum number of study centres should be equipped with the gadgets and services necessary for presentation of electronic media programmes. In view of the increasing role of technology in distance education, the equipment needed to be placed at maximum number of study centres of the University.
6. On Sundays and other days, study centre should conduct additional sessions only for presentation of audio and video programmes.
7. Media production facilities at the University headquarters should be increased in terms of technical personnel and modern equipment.
8. Interaction between academics, production staff, student support planners, should be more and continuous.
9. Rational decision-making on media components of courses should occur.
10. Coordination between AIR, Doordarshan and University on the role of media should occur.
11. Training in media planning and production for academics, production staff should be periodically organised with the help of EMPC, AIR, Doordarshan, MANA TV.
12. University should appoint a high level technical committee with media specialists and representatives of Akashvani and Doordarshan

to study the University's management of multiple media based distance education system and be benefited by its suggestions.

Golden Rules for Using Technology

Day to day technological facilities are increasing. Conscious efforts need to be made to use them in distance teaching. Bates suggests twelve golden rules for using technology in education:

1. Good teaching matters. Clear objectives, good structuring of learning materials, relevance to learner's needs, etc., apply to the use of any technology for teaching. Technology will never save bad teaching.
2. Each medium has a different range of production skills to exploit its unique features.
3. Technologies are generally flexible and interchangeable in education and training. Each technology can be used in a wide variety of ways.
4. All technologies have their strengths and weaknesses. There is no super technology.
5. All four media — print, audio, television, computer — should be made available for teaching purpose in one technological form or another.
6. A limited range of technologies covering all the main media should be used.
7. Through the use of appropriate technologies, high quality interaction with learning materials and between teachers and learners can be provided.
8. The number of learners to be served over the life of a course is a critical factor in technology selection.
9. New technologies are not necessarily better for teaching than old ones.
10. Teachers should be trained to use technologies effectively.
11. Subject experts, media specialists and instructional designers are essential on every course team.
12. Concentration should be on designing the learning experience and not on testing the technology.

11

Exposure to New Technological Initiatives

Now new technological developments are available to take education to students. Advanced countries are already making use of them for taking education to distance learners.

Nageswar Rao, Vice Chancellor of Uttarakhand Open University focused on the use of Open Educational Resources for distance education development in India. Following are the few recent initiatives mentioned by him.

a) ***National Programme on Technology Enhanced Learning (NPTEL):*** NPTEL was initiated in 2003 by seven IITs (Mumbai, Delhi, Kanpur, Kharagpur, Chennai, Guwahati and Roorkee) along with the Indian Institute of Science (IISc), Bengaluru, in 2003. In its First Phase (2003-2009), NPTEL developed 235 courses in web/ video format, at http:// nptel.iitm.ac.in (now defunct). In Phase II (2009-14), an additional 600 web and video courses were recorded, with new features, such as indexing and keyword search. A YouTube channel was created in this period. In Phase III, starting since 2014, an optional NOC (NPTEL Online Certification) was offered for Rs. 1,000 through a proctored exam, which has seen over one lakh registrations so far. Contents for the above courses were based on the model curriculum suggested by All India Council for Technical Education (AICTE). NPTEL is the most accessed library of peer-reviewed educational content in the world. Its YouTube channel, with close to 20,000 videos, has more than 800,000 subscribers and over 245 million views. Head-to-head, MIT OpenCourseware has more subscribers, but fewer than half the views (112 million views). Its content is also free to download, available on DVDs, and distributed under the CC BY-SA (Creative Commons Attribution-ShareAlike) license.

b) ***SWAYAM,*** Built on Open-edX by IIT Mumbai: It is a programme initiated by Government of India. The objective of this effort is to provide the best teaching learning resources to all. The courses hosted on SWAYAM are in four quadrants —

- Video lecture
- Specially prepared reading material that can be downloaded/ printed

- Self-assessment tests through tests and quizzes
- An online discussion forum for clearing the doubts.

c) ***Sakshat:*** It is an initiative of MHRD launched on 30 October 2006 to facilitate lifelong learning for students, teachers and those in employment, free of cost to them. The content development task for "SAKSHAT" was looked after by the Content Advisory Committee (CAC) for the respective subject, which consisted of representatives from educational institutions like Indira Gandhi National Open University (IGNOU), Delhi University, Kendriya Vidyalaya Sangthan (KVS), Navodyaya Vidyalaya Sangthan (NVS), National Institute of Open Schooling (NIOS) and National Council for Educational Research and Training (NCERT) and other prominent academicians in the field. The scheme is to provide connectivity to all institutions of higher learning to world of knowledge in the cyber space.

d) ***Ekalavya***: It is a project launched by IIT Mumbai in collaboration with National Mission for Education through ICT (NMEICT). The Ekalavya portal aims at a free exchange of knowledge and ideas, by placing all the relevant academic material in the Open Source, thus making considerable contribution to society. It aspires to build large collaborative communities where the requirements of knowledge seekers are matched with the initiatives of the knowledge providers.

e) ***National Science Digital Library***: It aims at providing comprehensive S&T information to students of science, engineering and technology in the country. Begun as a Tenth Five Year Plan Network Project of Council of Scientific and Industrial Research (CSIR), NSDL provides curriculum based content to address the information needs of the undergraduate students of science. Authored by eminent teachers and validated by renowned faculty in Indian universities and colleges, NSDL envisages to bring finest content to the students. The discussion forum has been provided for interactions amongst NSDL users.

f) ***e-PGPathshala and other initiatives:*** MHRD, under its National Mission on Education through ICT (NMEICT), has assigned work to the UGC for development of e-content in 77 subjects at postgraduate level. The content and its quality is the key component of education system. High quality, curriculum-based, interactive content in different subjects across all disciplines of social sciences, arts, fine arts and humanities, natural and mathematical sciences, linguistics and languages is being developed under this initiative

g) ***Consortium of Educational Communication (CEC)*** is an initiative of UGC. UG level e-content in 87 disciplines is available. National

Repository of Open Educational Resources (NROER) is an initiative of MHRD. The Repository is not just a collection of free and open digital resources, but it is much more. Resources are mapped to concepts that span the entire school and teacher education curricula of the country. FlexiLearn Open Course Portal is having more than 1000 open courses on the portal. There is course-wise registration and assessment. There is modular approach to earn course credits for obtaining a certificate, diploma or degree. Academic Advisors for each course are provided to learners.

h) ***Spoken Tutorial Project*** is developed by IIT Mumbai. It is about teaching and learning a particular FOSS (Free and Open Source Software) like Linux, Scilab, LaTeX, PHP and MySQL, Java, C/C++, LibreOffice etc. via an easy Video tool. Many of the Indian universities have signed MOU with Spoken Tutorial.

All these initiatives will strengthen the ODL system. ODL institutions must proactively use these initiatives for building a qualitative learner-centric framework.

12

Student Support

Composition of Student Support Services

There is no well established system of student support in distance education. It varies from institutions to institution. Many factors contribute to the development of a student support system. Each student support system in any distance teaching system is unique and what is provided in it depends on the market, aimed at the package which is employed, the delivery form, the status of the organisation and the socio-economic educational culture in which it operates. Student support services encompass a broad field and include admissions, registrations and records; examinations; information services; advising and counselling; and student advocacy and instructional support services. Support services in most distance education institutions include some or more of:

- class teaching at study centre
- individual tutorials at study centres or other locations
- annual residential schools (compulsory or optional) study of self help groups
- socio events
- counselling sessions at study centre
- correspondence with tutor and counsellor
- telephone contact with tutor and counsellor
- group telephone tutorials
- radio tutorials
- audio cassette correspondence
- computer mediated communication
- student newspapers

The popular and important forms of student support service are:

- Information support
- Guidance support
- Counsellsing support
- Tutorial support
- Library support

Information Support

Distance learners require many types of information about the institution they are studying with. In countries where the educational development level is low, the information requirements of distance learners are many and varied. In a conventional system of education, students need very minimum information, whereas in distance education which separates teachers from students, several types of information are required by students. Information is required before entering the institution and as well as during post entry. The distance education system being new, many people are not fully aware of the different dimensions of the system. The distance students are likely to carry with them to the system several wrong notions about the system prevalent in society. Hence, enough care is to be taken to provide proper information to the prospective students as well as students. Distance teaching institutions normally prepare and provide a variety of literature on the institution's goals, functions and processes. An important source of information is generally the institution's newsletter. In India, IGNOU and BRAOU bring out newsletter periodically. A newsletter can be an effective channel of communication between the university and its students.

Guidance Support

Guidance is a term with many meanings. Guidance is a continuous process of helping the individual's development to the maximum of his capacity in the direction most beneficial to himself and to society. Guidance involves help given by someone and is designed to assist a person to decide where he wants to go or how he can best accomplish his purpose.

Studying at a distance facilitates personal development which often generates a need for guidance on how to fulfill new ideas and educational aspirations. Distance students, particularly joining lower level courses, need guidance on course choice. Guidance is provide by a wide range of media.

Counselling Support

Counselling is "the advice, help and support given to students to enable them to make satisfactory progress in the system". The kind of role a counsellor might play in a distance system is illustrated by the following list of duties of counsellors:

- advising applicants,
- providing induction meetings for new students,
- explaining them distance learning system,

- advising students on course choice,
- giving guidance on problems of an administrative nature, such as payment of course fees, choice of summer schools, withdrawal from courses, late submission of written work, examinations, appeals,
- against tutor's grades, non-arrival of course materials,
- recording and monitoring of student progress and liaising with tutors,
- helping students to develop study skills,
- helping students to maintain motivation, and
- facilitating study-group activities.

Counselling is provided through different media in different distance education systems. The main media used for counselling are:

- Face to face counselling
- Group counselling
- Telephone counselling
- Counselling by letter
- Counselling by handbook
- Counselling by audio and video cassettes
- Counselling by broadcasting
- Counselling by computer

Library Support

There is an increasing recognition that student support services must include library services and library staff services. Library policies of different distance teaching universities in India and abroad vary from zero provision of books to elaborate library services. Foreign universities have the system comprising central library and libraries at study centres as we have in the Indian Open universities, but their library services are much more useful because they lend books through postal/ courier services and some of them provide Xeroxed copies of journal articles from the central library, without any additional charges. The Public Library system in Thailand is well organised and has become very popular by promoting distance education and by providing library and information services to adult learners.

Students as a Supporting Service

As important resource for student support is other students. The idea of peer group tutoring is a recent one. Students' organised groups can provide study group activities or supportive contact for isolated students. They are very useful for students in developing study skills and in over coming particular problems in the texts. Structuring and organising students groups is facilitated by some distance teaching system in the commencement of courses.

Tutorial Support

Tutoring is a course related support provided by an individual for a particular learner or group of learners who also use prepared materials as a resource. It takes various forms but is mainly facilitating the learning of a known group of learners and is not replacing the materials. It is generally provided by a local tutor with whom learners are in direct contact. What tutors actually do varies widely, and they may have different titles in different systems — trainee, tutor counsellor, learning advisor, academic counsellor, teacher mentor, teacher tutor and so on.

A look at the range of activities of tutors collected from a number of distance education institutions goes some way towards describing both what he does and the need for him to do it. The tutor's function include some or more of the following activities:

- Commenting on students' written work,
- marking/assigning grades to students' written work,
- helping students understand course materials through discussion,
- answering students queries about the system,
- helping students plan their work,
- organising self-help groups or study circles,
- conducting face-to-face or telephone discussions,
- teaching at a residential school or personal contact programme,
- keeping records of students' progress,
- giving a lecture,
- giving a feedback on course materials and student problems to the local centre co-ordinator or counsellor or course writers,
- negotiating with the institution on the students' behalf when certain problems occur.

Tutorials (a) provide appropriate help towards mastering the academic content of the course units by providing explanation, clarification and reinforcement of the teaching materials, (b) offer opportunity for and assistance towards improving basic and course specific study skills appropriate to the level of study, (c) enable students to express, explore, modify, balance and test their knowledge and their ideas through group activities, (d) encourage and stimulate the students' academic progress, and (e) prepare students to become independent learners.

In Open Universities in India, an academic counsellor called by different names attached to study centres, performs the functions of a tutor and a counsellor though the Coordinator who heads a study centre does counselling.

Student Support in BRAOU

The role and functions of Academic Counsellors of BRAOU are described in the Handbook for Academic Counsellors (1994). The Academic Counsellors are expected to undertake broadly four types of functions: (i) the tutorial function, (ii) the counselling function, (iii) the student evaluation function, and (iv) the feedback function:

(i) *Tutorial Function (Guiding the learners in the subject matter)*: The tutorial functions constitute the core of the Academic Counsellors' functions. These functions are subject specific and are provided mainly through face-to-face interaction sessions arranged at study centres. These tutorial functions include:

- clarifying subject matter related doubts and explaining difficult areas, concepts in the contact-cum-counselling sessions. It means the encapsulation of learning materials to suit the needs of different types of learners.
- encouraging the learners to read the learning materials on their own. The self instructional material provided to the learner is like a tutorial-in-print. The Academic Counsellor need not explain every aspect as is generally done in the conventional system.
- specifying the learning requirements of the subject and the ways in which they may be met.
- giving a holistic view of the entire course material and presenting it in a synoptic form to the learners when necessary. Updating of content where necessary especially when there is considerable time lag between the preparation and the presentation of the learning materials.
- helping the learners in identifying the printers' devils.
- helping the learners to relate the knowledge to their social context.
- enabling the learners to develop skills in the application of knowledge relevant to the programmes by conducting practicals, preparation of project reports and field work, etc. (particularly in technical, vocational and science programmes).
- assisting learners in making the best use of the audio-visual materials.

- acting as a resource person in intensive counselling sessions and special programmes (summer/ winter schools, etc.).

(ii) *Counselling Function (Advising and helping the learners in the study related and personal matters):* Counselling in education has been defined as 'the advice, help and support given to students to enable them to make satisfactory progress in the system'. The counselling functions of Academic Counsellors include:

- advice to learners on development of study skills.
- building the confidence of the learners in their ability to learn through the distance mode.
- eliminating the sense of isolation of distance learners by giving them a feeling that the institution is concerned about them.
- communication of general information about the system to the learners.
- giving general advice on courses of study, selection of optional, pace of study, time management, etc.
- sustaining the interest of the learner during the course.
- helping learners to plan and prepare assignment responses.
- guiding learners in preparing for examinations.

(iii) Student Evaluation Function (Assessment of assignments and year-end examination scripts): Academic Counsellors have an important role in making student evaluation an integral part of the learning process. They also play a key role in ensuring the validity and the reliability of the student assessment system. The functions of the Academic Counsellors in this area include:

- assessment of assignments to evaluate the learners' performance by giving detailed comments to make them a part of the learning process and a means of two way communication.
- assessment of year-end examination scripts to award credits to the learners' performance.
- helping the university in the conduct of examinations by acting as invigilators, observers etc.
- assessment of practicals, field reports, project reports, etc., (particularly in the case of science, technical and vocational programmes).

(iv) Feedback Function (Transmitting students' responses to learning material developers and delivery systems): The Academic Counsellors provide an important link between the university and the learner. They can help the university in making the system more learner-oriented. Some of the feedback functions of the Academic Counsellors are:

- to suggest to the university changes required in the content and format of learning materials based on the feedback from the learners.
- to suggest changes in the delivery systems to suit the needs of learners.
- to help the university in using learners' experience in the development of learning materials.
- to help the university in the contextualisation of the learning process.

Student Support in IGNOU

The Manual for Academic Counsellors of IGNOU clearly suggests several important tasks for Academic Counsellors in relation to the students. The following is the check list of tasks of the Academic Counsellors of IGNOU:

Helping towards mastering of units of courses

- Explaining difficult concepts from Units
- Discussing problems
- Arising in the counselling sessions
- Anticipated by the counsellor
- Unlearning/ discovering and correcting misconceptions.

Improving study skills

- Advising and giving examples of study methods
- Demonstrating skills and techniques
- Providing opportunities for individuals and group to practice
- Teaching students to use resources

Expanding knowledge through group activities

- Providing opportunities for students to work with each other
- Generating discussion, suggesting activities, setting problem
- Encouraging contribution from all students
- Ensuring suitable layout and maintaining a relaxed atmosphere.

Encouraging academic progress

- Relating students' experience and previous knowledge to course material
- Advising on programme of study
- Helping students to keep to schedules
- Presenting the course as something interesting and enjoyable

Developing independence

- 'Building up student self-confidence, motivation and moral strength
- Creating confidence in course material
- Encouraging self help activity

Early attention on improving basic study skills

- Note taking
- Essay writing
- Elementary mathematics
- How to learn from assignment comments

Other skills information

- How to make the best use of the IGNOU multi-media system
- Whom to contact when problems arise
- How to cope with them on one's own
- Analysis of the errors and deficiencies in TMAs
- Clear identification of the good points in TMAs
- The clearing up of problems, obscurities in the teaching materials
- Developing a fuller, more rounded understanding of the subject area than that provided by correspondence and other materials
- Human support and encouragement from tutor
- Advice on strategies for coping with materials and set tasks
- Understanding the main themes and issues for the course
- Help with preparation for the final examination
- Help with identifying my strengths and weaknesses as a student
- Discussion, practice in developing skills in argument
- Support, reassurance when depressed, worried about studies
- Help with pacing studies, identifying priorities

Regional Centres and Study Centres

In a distance teaching university, student support services are built on the concept of local centres. Local centres are normally of two kinds — regional centres and study centres.

The functions of regional centres in distance teaching universities include the following:

1. Enquiry, 2. Promotion, 3. Student Admissions, 4. Selection, appointment and supervision of part-time tutorial and counselling staff, 5. Training tutors and counsellors, 6. Organisation of special intensive/ mobile tutoring and counselling, 7. Organisation of weekend/ summer,

winter schools, residential schools, laboratory work, field work, etc., 8. Evaluation of assignments of students, 9. Conduct of examinations, 10. organisation of annual convocations, 11. Promotion of research on distance education, 12. setting up and maintenance of study centres, 13. Periodical meetings of coordinators and tutors, and academic counsellors, 14. Financial administration of study centres.

A study centre is known by different names in different teaching institutions. Resource centres, access centres, outreach centres and learning centres are some of the terms by which study centres are known in different places. The most popular name is study centre. The general characteristics of a study centre are:

- Shared space or reserved space in a local educational institution or non-educational organisation.
- Minimum equipment and facilities
- Local part-time staff
- Limited opening hours.

In most of the distance teaching instructions study centres are staffed by part-time staff. In some places full time staff operate. The head and his/ her supporting staff of a study centre are from different institutions .

Regional Services Division

The division dealing with student support services is known as the "Regional Services Division". It is responsible for the organisation, management and administration of regional centres and study centres all over the country. It also looks after the organisation of practicals, extended contact programmes, tele-conferencing sessions, counselling sessions, evaluation of assignment and conduct of the university examination, etc.

The responsibilities and functions assigned to the RSD are as follows:

- Organise and administer the national network of Regional and Study Centres for providing academic, administrative and information support services to students.
- Develop policies, systems and procedures in respect of establishment and management of Regional and Study Centres, their respective functionaries and the student services to be provided by them, and also undertake periodical review in the light of new developments/ demands on the system.
- Negotiate with Government Departments, educational institutions, other organisations including voluntary organisations for establishment of new Regional and Study Centres.

- Assess availability of physical facilities and academic expertise and arrange the delivery of all academic programmes launched by the university after developing in consultation with respective schools, necessary norms, procedures and payment structures.
- Identify and appoint suitable persons as academic counsellors for counselling, practicals and evaluation of assignments.
- Organise orientation programmes for academic counsellors as well as other part-time functionaries of Study Centres.
- Organise induction and in-service training programmes for full-time staff of Regional Centres
- Funding and expenditure control of Regional and Study Centres.
- Provide necessary furniture and equipments to Regional and Study Centres.
- Coordinate with schools and divisions at the headquarters on various matters related to students support services in general and Regional and Study Centres in particular.
- Attend to student queries, problems and grievances.
- Monitor all operations at Regional and Study Centres and provide feedback to Schools about academic activities including counselling, practicals, audio-video sessions and alignment evaluation.
- Coordinate teleconferencing activity in Regional and Study Centres.
- Promote the university's programmes in regions, conduct admission procedure at all Regional Centres and arrange transfer of admission data to SRE Division and remittance of fee collection to the Finance Division.

To provide student support services and for delivery of programmes, a Diversified Delivery System has been designed comprising of a vast network of Regional and Study Centres. There are different types of study centres based on the needs of the learners and nature of the programmes. This institutional network makes best use of computer networking, electronic media and modern communication technologies.

13
Staff Development

Staff development is one of the priority activities of a distance teaching system. In most of the countries a large number of personnel in distance education institutions are drawn from the conventional education system and hence training becomes imperative for equipping them with necessary knowledge, skills: and aptitudes to perform the new tasks in new systems.

The need for training distance educators is well expressed by the UNESCO Regional Office for Education in Asia and Pacific in the following words, "...the lack of trained personnel is a stumbling block. Most of the people, working in distance education have come from formal system and are attending to the methods of traditional education. Their new roles demand a new set of skills and attitudes, personnel must be reoriented and retrained for their changed task ...."

There are several theoretical and practical objectives of staff development. The Commonwealth of Learning (COL) Round Table Conference on Training (1990), emphasising the importance of adequately trained manpower to improve the quality of distance education stated that training programme should:

- suit needs of the institution.
- be available to all categories of staff.
- suit the experience of the staff.
- provide a sequence of training opportunities.
- offer scope for career advancement.
- employ a variety of strategies.

Staff development is the new term for training in distance education literature. Staff development refers to the acquisition of knowledge and skills that people who work in distance education system need. As highlighted by Prasad, the training of staff is an essential requirement of distance education system because:

- distance education is a relatively new field and most of the staff who come from the formal system need orientation to distance education.
- training facilitates the updating of existing knowledge and acquisition of new knowledge, new skills and positive attitudes are required for the job.

- training is a tool for staff development which refers to harmonising the individual and institutional goals.
- training results in more competence to do the job, resulting in more job satisfaction to staff.
- training builds up the capabilities for taking higher responsibilities thus paving the way for career advancement.
- training results in greater commitment on the part of the staff.
- training staff contributes to the better performance of the institution resulting in a better image, credibility and viability of the system.
- training is an effective mechanism to meet the needs and challenges of the information age.
- staff training is necessary for the adoption of new technologies.
- staff training provides a frame of reference for work.
- staff training provides opportunities for self development and learning from experience.
- staff training is necessary to enable the institution to face the challenges of change.
- staff training provides trainees an overall view of the system and helps them in relating their role to the system.
- staff training results in better services to the students.
- the training of policy makers, educators and public men lends social support to the system.

Categories of Staff in Distance Systems

In higher distance education system several categories of staff perform varied tasks. Rumble, a keen observer of the Open University functioning, identified different categories of staff and their functions. All these categories of staff need training and retraining from time to time for effective and efficient performance of their tasks.

Staff Categories in Distance Education Systems

Function	*Categories of Staff*
General Management	Head of institution, departmental heads, and personal assistants and secretaries to these, planners with statisticians and other support staff, project control staff, institutional evaluators
Secretariat	Administrators (policy formulation and committee secretaries), secretaries/ typists, filing clerks
Personnel	Personnel officers concerned with recruitment training, industrial relations, terms and conditions of service, establishment control, secretaries and clerks
Management Services	Systems analysts, programmers, computer centre managers, input clerks, etc.
Finance	Professional staff and supporting clerks concerned with accounts, staff payments, creditor payments, fees administration, financial planning, budgetary control, purchasing, some secretaries
Buildings and Estates	Buildings and estate planner, surveyor, services engineer, staff connected with utilities and services (plumbers, electricians, painters, carpenters), security guards, porters and internal mail staff, gardeners
Public Relations	Press and publicity officers, secretaries, house newspaper editor, etc.
Catering	Kitchen staff, serving staff, etc.
Materials development, Production and Operational Presentation	Coordination by course or project leader, aided by project administrator, (and by scheduling and other professional staff as needed)
Library	Librarians
All materials	Curriculum planners, subject experts, educational technologists
Print	Editors, typists, word processor operators, designers, graphic artists and photographers, copyeditors
Broadcasts and audio-visual	Producers, script-writers
Computer Assisted learning	Programmers
Home Experiments	Technicians to design equipment
Tuition and Assessment	Senior tutors
Material Production	
Print	Editors, typesetters, printers

Broadcasts/ AV	Designers, visual effects, model building and science construction staff, costume and make up staff, floor managers, studio assistants, camera crews, sound recordists, film and sound editors, announcers, presenters, actors, copyeditors, transport staff, etc.
Home Experiments	Production staff, assembly staff, technicians (to test equipment)
Computer Assisted Learning	Technicians
Materials Storage and Distribution	Generally store men, packers, and dispatch clerks
Students Administration and Teaching	For broadcasts on open and closed circuit transmission: appropriate staff concerned with their transmission. For computer assisted instruction operational and computer centre staff.
Administration	Administration, admission and student records clerks student enquiry service clerks Examination administration, examinations and assignment clerks. Regional and/ or local centre administration, secretaries and clerks, security guards, cleaners, etc.
Training	Senior tutors and counsellors, tutors, demonstrators counsellors, examination invigilators and script makers, etc.

Tasks and Training Needs of Staff

A Regional Seminar organised by UNESCO Regional office for Education in Asia and Pacific attempted to identify different broad categories of personnel, their respective tasks and their training needs. Since the different categories of distance education personnel working in different countries are not exactly the same and do not operate or interact in one and the same manner, only broad categories of personnel, their tasks and training needs have been spelled out accordingly. Various personnel working in distance education are categorised by UNESCO seminar under four heads as follows:

a) policy makers, planners, administrators and researchers.
b) Personnel relating to the production of correspondence materials.
c) personnel relating to production of radio broadcasts.
d) personnel relating to production of TV programmes.

Skills Required by Staff

In the preceding sections, various categories of personnel are identified. Consequently, their task specifications and training needs were also spelled out.

As there are many personnel needing different skills, it is highly impossible to draw up specific training programmes for each category. However, training programmes can be envisaged at two levels: one to provide general information about distance education and the second to provide specific skill competencies for different jobs. The general course can be called the "Foundations and Skills" course and the job specifics, 'Options'. The foundation course may take between 25 and 35 hours and options between 50 to 60 hours. The foundation and options courses can also be designed at two levels, one for personnel working in distance education institutions and other for field workers.

Strategies for Staff Development

Most strategies used for staff development in the conventional systems of education are used for distance education systems also. The following are the popular strategies used for staff development.

- Workshops
- Field Staff Programmes
- Manuals
- Professional Associations
- In-House Programmes
- Assistance from Resource Institutions
- Consultancy
- Attachments
- Visits
- Adoptions

Staff Training and Research Institute of Distance Education (STRIDE)

The Staff Training and Research Institute of Distance Education (STRIDE) started as the Division of Distance Education in 1986, soon after the establishment of IGNOU in 1985, to cater to the training needs of various functionaries of the Indira Gandhi National Open University (IGNOU).

Later, based on the proposal by the Commonwealth of Learning (COL), Asian Development Bank (ADB) and Ministry of Human Resource Development (MHRD), to the Government of India to set up a training and research institute for distance education in the South Asian Region, the Division of Distance Education of IGNOU was upgraded into the Staff Training and Research Institute of Distance Education in 1993.

STRIDE has been conducting staff development and research activities for IGNOU, State Open Universities (SOUs) and Distance Education Institutes (DEIs) in India as well as serving the distance education training, research and capacity building needs of around 45 Asian, African and the Caribbean countries. More than 700 major training programmes have been conducted by STRIDE since its inception.

STRIDE has brought out the following Handbooks on different dimensions of DE use as for resource material for staff training programmes.

1. Open and Distance Education
2. Effective Learning
3. Academic Counselling in ODL
4. Assessment and Evaluation in DE
5. Development and Revision of SLM
6. Editing in DE
7. Media and Technology in DE
8. E-Learning
9. Learner Support Service in DE
10. Cost Analysis in ODL
11. Programmes Evaluation in ODE
12. Psychological Skills for ODL
13. Staff Development in ODE
14. DE: Opportunities for Northeast Learners
15. Servicing Students with Disabilities in DE

CSTD (BRAOU)

BRAOU set up, in April 1993, a separate unit under the name Centre for Staff Training and Development (CSTD). The functions of the Centre are:

- assessment of training needs of different categories of distance educators.
- planning and organisation of training programmes for different categories of distance educators such as:
- policy makers/ planners/ administrators, course writers, editors, assessors, academic counsellors, coordinators, and other staff of student support services, audio-visual staff, administrative staff, support staff, technical staff, research and evaluation staff, and training the trainers.

- training programmes for the application of new technologies in distance education.
- collaboration with other institutions with common aims.
- consultancy services and organisation of need-based and custom built training programme in educational management/ administration.

CSTD has so far organised several training programmes. Later, CSTD was merged with GRADE.

G. Ram Reddy Research Academy in Distance Education (GRADE)

Considering the contemporary development in open and distance learning, research is highly essential for professional development. The research outcome helps in enhancing the quality of teaching and learning. It also examines the strategies and policies implemented by distance educators to see if they meet the characteristics and needs of the distance learners. In order to benefit the open and distance learning systems, BRAOU has set up a Research Academy of Distance Education named after Ram Reddy, the founder Vice-Chancellor of the University. The objectives of the academy are:

- to carry out system-based research in distance education in India, Asian Region and beyond.
- to conduct workshops, seminars and training programmes.
- to establish collaboration with institutions and agencies in India and abroad.
- to undertake consultancy services and commission projects related to the distance education system.
- to promote, coordinate, fund and sponsor research projects.
- to publish research work in the field of distance education and to establish and maintain a data bank.
- to receive grants, scholarships, endowments and other donations.
- to institute awards, endowments and prizes.
- to grant fellowships.
- to enter into exchange programmes with distance education institutions.

The Academy would help to formalise and collate all academic efforts so as to encourage research studies, which would greatly enhance the quality of distance education.

GRADE caters to the needs of distance teaching institutions, distance educators, researchers, policy makers, organisations and institutions with research interests for promoting distance education. Its specific functions are geared to match the requirements of the above target groups.

GRADE produced the following material to serve the purpose of training material:

1. Development of Curriculum and Learning Material
2. Learner Service: Quality Parameters
3. Planning and Design of Academic Programmes
4. Open Distance Learning in AP
5. Development of Audio-Visual and Computer Aided Learning Materials and Research
6. Management of Learner Assessment and Evaluation
7. House and Print Style Manual

14

System Evaluation

Indian distance education systems are rarely evaluated by researchers. Evaluation is done mostly by government agencies as and when government felt in the context of criticism by educational planners and organisations. Indian distance educators have not evolved criteria relevant to the evaluation of distance teaching systems. Indian distance educators and researchers could have benefited by the works of scholars like Gooler, Keegan, Rumble, McIntosh, Kemmis, etc. Let us see the criteria suggested by above writers and practitioners of distance education.

Gooler suggested the following seven criteria.

- Equality of opportunity: the extent to which distance education contributes to equality of educational opportunities
- Access: the extent to which distance education provides access to home-based adults.
- Relevancy to needs and expectations: the extent to which distance education provides opportunities and services that are regarded as being of priority to communicate in general, or to specific individuals, and particularly where there are a number of potential target audiences with differing needs.
- Quality of the programme offerings: the quality of the educational materials and their content in comparison with traditional Systems. The quality of design and the ease with which persons obtain access to the materials may also be considered.
- Learner outcomes: the extent to which students achieve the goals which are set for them, or which they set for themselves. A distinction can be made here between students who gain a formal qualification set by the university (such as a degree), and those who, while apparently dropping out mid-way through their studies, have in fact accomplished everything they want to do.
- Cost-effectiveness: the extent to which distance-education programmes are cost-effective, involving a study of the relative cost of the programme vis-a-vis conventional programmes in terms of the unit cost per graduate, per student participating, or per credit-hour earned. Valid measures of effectiveness are, however, very difficult to obtain.

- Impact: the impact which the programme has on institutions, other programmes and individuals, and particularly the way in which a distance education programme has influenced their goals, policies and directions; the extent to which traditional institutions or programmes are led to experiment with new media, or to operate with distance teaching institutions in the production of materials or courses; and the extent to which they may adjust their academic regulations to allow, for example, transferability of credit between the distance teaching programme and their own programme; Finally, a distance education programme may have an impact on its students and on society as a whole, for example, by bringing an increased awareness of health care as a result of a particular course or series of courses, or by increasing awareness of the educational needs of adults.
- Generation of knowledge: the extent to which distance education contributes knowledge useful to a better understanding of the learning process.

Four Point Criteria of Keegan and Rumble

Keegan and Rumble appraised the success or failure of nine DTUs using a four-point assessment scheme: (1) the quality of the learning achieved, (2) the quantity of learning achieved, (3) the status of the learning achieved, and (4) the relative cost of the learning achieved. Keegan recommended the four point evaluation for the overall evaluation of any distance teaching system.

The sub-criteria under each of the four main criteria used by Keegan and Rumble are as follows:

1. The quantity of the learning achieved
    - the success of the system in widening access, not just in terms of absolute numbers, but in attracting specific target groups;
    - drop outs;
    - the quantity of the output relative to the input (the output/ input ratio);
    - the time it takes to produce the output; and
    - the system's success in satisfying national local and individual needs.

To receive a satisfactory evaluation, the institution is required to achieve measurable success in: (i) the avoidance of avoidable drop out; (ii) the number of successful students as a proportion of the number of students admitted; and (iii) the time it takes for students to achieve successful outcomes.

2. The quality of learning achieved—Under this heading are considered:
   - the quality of the learning materials provided by the distance system; .
   - the extent to which distance teaching is a suitable vehicle for educating students in certain subjects;
   - the extent to which education is provided as opposed to instruction;
   - the effectiveness of learning at a distance; and
   - the "inter subjectivity" of learning at a distance.
3. The status of the learning achieved—Under this heading are considered:
   - the extent to which other educational institutions recognise the studies for credit transfer purposes;
   - the acceptance of the degrees and diplomas awarded as qualifying students to go on to higher level studies;
   - the recognition of the awards by employers; and
   - the esteem in which the distance teaching institutions and their awards are held in the community at large.
4. The relative cost of the learning achieved—Under this are considered:
   - the cost efficiency of distance universities relative to conventional universities or to other modes of internal operation which the distance universities could adopt;
   - the cost effectiveness of distance universities relative to conventional universities — the concept of cost effectiveness tries to weigh the relative value of the outputs in qualitative terms;
   - the cost benefits of distance and traditional university education, in which the costs of the education provided and the benefits (direct and indirect, financial and social) to the individual and society are taken into account; and
   - the opportunity cost of education at a distance.

Other Criteria

There are other criteria by which activities and programmes of Distance Teaching Intuitions could be evaluated. McIntosh, Kemmis, and Rumble are prominent among those who provided different criteria of assessment of effectiveness of distance education.

McIntosh emphasises formative evaluation, defined as evaluation that is conducted in conjunction with the development of a new educational programme with the aim of influencing that develops.

Kemmis suggests four levels of evaluation: (1) programme evaluation, concerning general institutional relationships, (2) curriculum evaluation, concerning the educational arrangements of whole curricula and particular courses, (3) evaluation of student, concerning the opportunities for learning created by a particular teaching/ learning encounter, and (4) students assessments, concerning the outcomes of student learning.

Rumble basing on Gooler's criteria but taking into account various criteria suggested by others provides an evaluative analysis of distance education institutions on the seven criteria: (1) access, (2) relevancy to needs and expectations, (3) quality of programmes offered, (4) learner outcomes, (5) effectiveness and efficiency, (6) impact, and (7) generation of knowledge.

Performance Indicators

In recent years considerable interest is developing in the development of performance indicators as an aid to educational management and as a means of assessing the overall performance of an institution. Many now feel that there should be a series of performance indicators that can be used in non profit making service organisations like distance teaching universities to measure the effective and efficient-accomplishment of

Performance Indicators as Applied to Distance Education

Accessibility	Hours of opening of local study centres, broadcast transmission hours, access media in the home
Extensiveness	Student enrolments against target Numbers/ quotas, number of users of special services, percentage use of media
Appropriateness	Demand for courses/Service; mismatch between demand and availability
Efficiency	Cost per service per student per course, etc.
Effectiveness	Comparison of planned to actual; Percentage utilising facility or service; graduate success in employment, etc. budgeted to actual cost; planned to actual cost per student course; planned to actual wastage rates
Acceptability	Demand for courses, number of complaints about course content or services, complaints about speed for service.
Outcomes/ Benefits/Impacts	Increased earning power of ex-students/ graduates, benefits to society, local community, other educational institution

the expectations of the institution's constituencies. Sorenson and Grove worked on 'Cost-outcome and Cost-effectiveness Analysis: Emerging Non Profit Performance, Evaluations Techniques' indicated several service performance indicators. Of these the significant ones are availability, awareness, acceptability, accessibility, appropriateness extensiveness, efficiency, effectiveness and outcomes benefits/ impacts. Rumble ably summarised each of these service performance indicators by applying to distance education

Taking into consideration various criteria suggested by distance educators and writers, a set of criteria appropriate to Indian conditions to appraise the performance of Indian distance higher education systems with particular reference to open universities is evolved by some Indian distance educators. The suggested criteria include:

- Relevancy to needs and expectations of people
- Availability of courses
- Extensiveness
- Quality of courses offered
- Effectiveness and efficiency
- Learner outcomes
- Access
- Impact
- Generation of knowledge.

15

Framework for Ranking

The process of framing the National Institutional Ranking Framework (NIRF) began in October 2014 with the constitution of a committee under the chairmanship of Secretary, Ministry of HRD. The terms of the committee are to suggest a reliable, transparent and authentic national framework for performance measurement, ranking of institutions for higher education and to recommend institutional mechanisms, processes and timelines for implementation of the NIRF. The framework was given a final shape subsequent to intense discussions and deliberations in a series of meetings of the committee and exchange with stakeholders through many discussions. The NIRF envisaged separate ranking for different categories of institutions. The final framework identified 22 parameters under five major heads, several of them are similar to those employed globally, such as excellence in teaching, learning and research. Rankings are made for Engineering, Management, Pharmacy and University sectors. Distance education institutions are not covered by the ranking process.

A broad-based framework consisting of quality parameters in DE institutions in India is needed, in view of the increasing number of DE institutions in the country. The Distance Education Bureau of UGC mentioned the number of approved universities and institutions providing higher distance education during 2016-17 as 108. Madhava Menon Committee (2009-10) in its report observed that "about 11 per cent of the total enrolled students in ODL system is in the range of 15 per cent-20 per cent in State open universities and around 30 per cent in DEIs..." The AISHE Report for 2015-16 mentions 11.05 per cent enrollment in distance education.

Prior to 2013, Distance Education (DE) system was under the regulatory control of Distance Education Council (DEC) under the administrative control of IGNOU. The Ministry of HRD issued direction in December 2012 to give the regulatory functions with regard to DE programmes in higher education under the direct control of UGC through Distance Education Bureau constituted in May 2013. This is an interim measure till Distance Education Council of India is created by the Parliament.

Proposal Model Framework of ODL Institutions

Sanjay Tiwari of Directorate of Distance Education, Guru Jambheshwar University of Science and Technology, suggested a broad model framework for ranking distance education in India on the variables shown in the following table (*University News*, 18-24 September 2017)

Proposed Model Framework for Ranking of ODL in India

Infrastructure	**Teaching Learning Resources**	**Curriculum Design and Development**	**ICT**
– Physical (Space, Location, Building, etc.) – Digital infrastructure – Human resources – Supporting Infrastructure	– Faculty – Pedagogy – Study Material – Instructional Design – Learning Modules – E-library – E-lecturing – Delivery Mode – Research and extension – Feedback	– Programmes Structure and design – Modular Courses – Course recognition and standardisation – Course Updating – Academic Autonomy – Market Friendliness	– Online processes – Digital Delivery – ICT enabled teaching – learning and evaluation – E-Resources
Regulation	**Student Support Service**	**Collaboration**	**Outreach and Inclusivity**
– Jurisdiction – Degree of compliance with Regulators (UGC, DEC, AICTE, etc) – Institutional recognition – Programme recognition – Certificate of standardisation	– Clientele – Demography – Diversity – Admission Process – Eligibility Criteria – Fee structure – Self-Learning Material (SLM) – Counselling – Personal Contact Programmes (PCPs) – Administration – Credit Transfer – Grievance Handling Mechanisms – Internal Assessment – Consistent Evaluation – Examination – Degree Distribution, etc	– Degree of collaboration with national, international and regional institutions – Sharing of Teaching Learning resources – Credit Transfer and Lateral Entry – Students Exchange Programmes – Faculty Exchange Programmes – Project Based Study	– Community Development – Diversity of students – Geographical spread of learners – Participation of Women, – SC, ST, OBC, Minority, Differently Abled People or Divyangs in ODL, etc.

Governance and Leadership	**Stakeholders Perception**	**Education Outcome and Employability**	**Funding**
– Vision, Mission, Objectives – Governance Structure – Quality Policy – Internal Quality Assurance – Academic Leadership – Administration Leadership	– Employers Perception – Public Perception – Peer Perception – Society Perception	– Placements – Entrepreneurial Development – Employability Potential of skill based courses	– Funding from external – Agencies – Government Support – Institutional Funding – Corporate Funding – Internally generated Funds – Self Financing – Utilisation of funds in development of ODL

16

Survey of Research

Research is a critical and creative activity undertaken on systematic discipline basis and dedicated to increasing knowledge. Research can contribute to knowledge through discoveries or innovative ideas and techniques, conceptual refinements or constructive critiques and syntheses.

The tradition of research in Indian distance education is not very strong and sound. In fact, only after the establishment of IGNOU in 1985, research activity began. Practically for about two decades from the beginning of correspondence courses in Conventional Universities, research was of low priority.

Distance education is a branch of general education and therefore distance education research and practices have been influenced by research on adult learning.

M.B. Buch was the pioneer in the field of educational research in India (1974 to 1991). All the researches on distance education were included in the fifth survey (1971-92). In the fifth survey of Educational Research, the studies on distance education dealt with enrollment trends courses growth, needs and characteristics of learners, development of course materials instructional strategies, economics, evaluation of the system etc. covering the period from 1971 to 1992. The survey was confined to 58 research studies

The report of the Madhava Menon Committee to suggest measures to regulate education through distance mode stated that distance education research has grown. It says:

"Research and development forms the backbone of any system in order to bring in quality and standards. Being a dynamic system driven by societal, economic and technological changes, ODL has been changing rapidly and dramatically. The changing technological environment of distance education and paradigm shift affecting it needs to be periodically reviewed. Also the growing acceptance of open and distance learning system in our country and the innovations being an integral part of the ODL system it has become imperative to evaluate the system periodically. There is ample proof of growth of distance education research which is evident from the increasing number of journals, seminars, workshops, symposia, etc. analysing the growth of the system" (Government of India, 2011).

Broadly research in distance education has been classified into the following heads:

1. Growth of DE policy, planning and management
2. Programmes and Courses
3. Distance learners
4. Course development and evaluation
5. Output and impact of DE
6. Instructional process
7. Economics of DE.

Most of the research studies in distance education in India are descriptive in nature and not research studies in the real sense. Some attempts have been made by some writers to classify and review research studies in distance education in India. Among those who analysed and reviewed studies, the prominent ones are Arun Gupta and Renu Arun (1986), Sujatha (1988), Panda (1992), Sahoo (1992), Satyanarayana (1996), Panda, Satyanarayana and Sharma (1996), Murali Manohar (1996), Lokesh Koul (1997, 2006), Pushpa Ramakrishna and Prasad (1999) Sanjay Mishra (2002), Satyanarayana and Sesharatham (2004), Subbarao (2004).

Arun Gupta and Renu Arun (1986) classified the contributions of Indian writers to distance education till the advent of the Open University system in India into eleven categories and critically observed:

- A significant number of contributions happened to be the addresses of the VIPs in education circles in different committees, conferences and workshops. In other words, these writings were primarily meant for the consumption of a particular audience/target group and can be described as the speeches/papers of the hour. At best, these reflected the current thinking of the organisations/ departments to which the writers belonged and did not reflect a serious attempt to grapple with the issues from academic and research angles. No wonder the impact of these writings was marginal.
- There existed no specialised journal/publication/ newsletter exclusively devoted to the dissemination of latest thoughts and practices in the field of distance education at the regional, state or national levels.
- A significant proportion of the literature devoted to the description or explanation of distance education, its concepts, underlying principles, problems and difficulties especially in the domain of higher education as also the ramifications of distance education in the context of developing countries.

A good deal of duplication in the content could be observed in these contributions. A significant characteristic of literature was relative ignorance of the writers about concurrent thinking. Another feature was a relative absence of critical attitude in dealing with the different issues.

- Contributors mostly belonged to the community of distance educators in the universities. The published work was comparatively much less. This resulted in lack of incisive, comparative and analytic treatment of the formal education and lacked depth and insight into the whole issue from the academic angle.
- Distance learners, their problems, characteristics, learning styles, drop out and completion rates, evaluation and assessment and overall satisfaction from distance learning programmes had not gained the attention of Indian writers. This clearly indicated that the target groups for whom distance education programmes were offered and their subsequent satisfaction from these programmes were never considered factors of importance.
- The fields of vocational and professional education remained outside the purview of writers. The academic fraternity in India largely upheld that distance education was an unsuitable medium for technical, vocational, professional and recurrent education.
- Research efforts remained fragmentary and isolated. Researches on distance education were very few in number. From the points of theoretical value and technical designs, the studies lacked rigour.

Summing up the state of the art, the authors commented "the Indian contributions to distance education fall short of the expected standard to give a new direction and vitality to distance education". They hoped that the future would witness more significant and constructive contributions, both theoretical and empirical, from the Indian distance educators and experts to give a new lease of life to distance education, thereby enabling the nation to benefit from this channel of education and solve some of its gigantic problems.

In 1988 the National Institute of Educational Planning and Administration, (now NUEPA), New Delhi, organised a Workshop on Research in Distance Education and Educational Technology with the following objectives:

- to review the status and trends of research in distance education and educational technology,

- to identify problems, and priority areas for research in planning and management of distance education and educational technology,
- to prepare research proposals on identified research problems, and
- to develop a network of effort of research support to planning and management of distance education and educational technology.

Sujatha (1988) in her presentation to the Workshop classified the research works of the decade 1976-86 into nine areas and commented on them the following way:

- From the point of view of methodological aspects, most of the studies were descriptive highlighting the status and functioning of the system, exploring facts and figures related to its different dimensions.
- Except a few exploratory studies, most of the studies on distance education were evaluative in nature.
- Most of the evaluation studies were piecemeal in form and did not take into account the context of the functioning of the system.
- The research studies pointed that the instructional materials supplied to the students were designed mostly in an unscientific way and presented in an essay type manner, thus lacking pedagogy of self-learning.

She concluded that studies are "too few, too dispersed and yet too inadequate to derive proper feedback for planning and management of the system on a scientific basis".

Sahoo (1992) classified the studies into nine broad categories and on the basis of his review suggested the following areas for large scale research:

- Development of courses on the basis of appropriate planning and need assessment.
- Formulation of appropriate strategies of instruction of different courses.
- Utilisation of technology in distance education.
- Economics of distance education.
- All issues concerning the open school system and open university system.
- Structure and style of management of distance education.

Panda (1992) attempted an analysis of 142 research studies under nine areas, dividing each area into two sub-categories of correspondence education and Open University education. He suggested the following broad areas for urgent attention of researchers:

- Curriculum planning and development.
- Different ways/ models of developing courses/ multi media packages and testing the instructional components of these packages for wide implementation.
- Instructional design, development and implementation.
- Activities and experiences of distance learners.
- Development of model of coordination, information dissemination and exchange and quality control within the process of distance education activities.
- Development of models of planning and management, organisation and financial decision making separately for different types of institutions.

Murali Manohar, Sudhakar and Rajendra Prasad (1996) conducted a bibliographic study covering 1176 works on distance education in India available during the previous three decades. The works included Government Reports, University Projects Reports, Review Committees' Reports, Periodical Features, University Publicity Materials, etc. The authors classified the works under 15 heads. They found that seventy five per cent of the works were descriptive and informative and only twelve per cent were empirical.

The main observation made by the reviewers was that minor dimensions of the distance education system were studied neglecting the major aspects of the system. They pointed that there were hardly any theoretical or conceptual developments in field and no proper lessons could be learnt from the practice and formulations based on empirical realities. They concluded that there is hardly any serious study in India that would be able to stand as a testimony to create confidence in the system.

Finally the reviewers called for (a) thorough review of research already done, (b) identification of thrust areas for future research, documentation and library services, (c) creation of research and evaluation cells in all CCIs/OUs, (d) coordination at the national level between UGC, IGNOU (DEC and STRIDE), ICSSR, NUEPA and other promoting and funding agencies, and (e) formulation of a national research policy on distance education in India.

The status of research activity in distance education in Andhra Pradesh was reviewed by Sesharatnam (1996). Her observations are still valid. She felt that:

- research efforts have been fragmentary and isolated; from the point of view of theoretical value and design. The research activity leaves much to be desired,
- most of the studies conducted so far have focused on issues at the micro level; most of the studies conducted so far are a few and are descriptive in nature highlighting the status and functioning of the system with fact and figures, and
- maintaining quality in spread of distance education does not seem to the concern of distance educators.

Panda, Satyanarayana and Shanna (1996) in their pioneering work *Open and Distance Education Research: Analysis and Annotation* reviewed quite a sizeable number of studies on open and distance education in India. They analysed over 152 studies and annotated 88 studies of them. The studies covered included some published and some unpublished, some institutionally sponsored and some individually undertaken, some projects and some dissertations at universities, open universities and open schools. They analysed studies under nine sub-themes and also listed in the references almost all the research studies considered on Indian distance education. Analysing the studies, the authors expressed three concerns:

- The first concern is with regard to the 'comprehensiveness' of most of the studies, i.e., barring a few studies, there is lack of compatibility between the macro and micro issues and lack of a proper theoretical base to back them up.
- The second concern is with regard to the 'methodology' of research. Only a few studies are methodologically sound, and most of the studies are either descriptive status surveys or experimental studies with poor methodological procedures.
- The third concern is with regard the 'coverage' of the research problems selected by the researchers. "Only a few studies could be considered holistic, appropriate, and generalisable. Investigating a problem for the sake of either conducting a study in the area of distance education or getting a degree has no meaning whatsoever." Even research studies conducted in distance education from 1992 to 1994 have neither changed the characterisation of the issues raised above nor significantly contributed to the quality of research.

Pushpa Ramakrishna and Prasad (1999) identified 17 thrust areas for research in distance education:

1. Philosophy and concepts.
2. History of Distance Education.

3. Aims/ Goals/ Mission of institutions.
4. Programme Planning and Curriculum Design.
5. Development of Learning Materials (Print and Non-print).
6. Teaching and Learning Processes.
7. Student Support Services and Delivery Systems.
8. Student Evaluation (Formative and Summative).
9. System Programme Evaluation (Formative and Summative).
10. Economics of Distance Education.
11. Media in Distance Education.
12. Management of the System.
13. Application of New Technologies.
14. Open Education Network, National and international.
15. Quality Assurance.
16. Research Methodologies in Distance Education.
17. Staff Training and Development.

Sanjay Mishra (2002) analysed the first 10 volumes of *Indian Journal of Open Learning* and concluded that several gaps exist in the research literature. He particularly pointed out the areas of design and development of self learning materials. Lokesh Koul (2006) after briefly reviewing research studies conducted in the last four decades concluded that the trend of research on distance education in terms of its quality and depth has not been encouraging. His analysis of research studies revealed the following significant features:

- The research studies did not show any qualitative trend with respect to theory and practice of distance education.
- The specific causes of huge enrollment or dropout in different courses/ institutions among various categories of distance learners have not been studied in any of the researches.
- Research studies have mostly adopted descriptive survey approach and quantitative analysis techniques.
- Impact and intervention studies and evaluation of distance education system have been ignored.
- The teachers associated with distance education courses in conventional universities have hardly provided any orientation in the theory and practice of distance education programmes.
- While analysing various issues and problems of distance education the researches have used the research processes and techniques as practised in conventional system. Distance education research has unique problems which are quite different from the research of conventional system.

Lokesh Koul (2006) strongly felt that research must be able to:

- generate knowledge on various components of distance education; theory and its relevance with respect to different dimensions of Indian society, process and product, and cost effectiveness,
- help practitioners in the distance education system to encapsulate their experiences for the benefit of the system and future researchers,
- identify the underlying issues of learner characteristics and needs,
- study the influence of media upon the instructional system,
- focus on the issue of equity of access to interactive delivery systems,
- identify the roles of teachers, counsellors/ facilitator, and student in the distance education process,
- contribute to the emergence of distance education as a discipline,
- strengthen the morale of the distance education community in the country and help attract talent to this emerging area, and
- providing results of empirical researches with regard to the potential of distance education to ensure high quality and relevant education to a large number of needy learners at a reasonable cost.

To achieve these objectives he suggested that IGNOU and UGC at the tertiary level, NIOS and NCERT at the school level may undertake the responsibility of commissioning and assisting research projects jointly so that the two systems formal/ conventional and the distance/ open could come together.

Rekkedal in his richly documented essay *Research in Distance Education* pointed to some challenges for the future of distance education research and to some possible recommendations and actions:

- Distance education needs different kinds of research. As an applied professional field, it needs both basic research which tests and develops knowledge to guide practice, and it needs research to solve practical problems.
- Cooperation on research might give better results than individual based projects.
- Integration of research philosophies, methods and designs would benefit the development of theory and practice in distance education.
- Professionals and managers in distance education need to have some training in research methods, statistics and basic problems

concerned with generalisations, validity and reliability of results from empirical research.
- There is a large need for research on how different students learn with different kinds of technology in different types of programmes. Research should be driven by educational theory rather than by the general enthusiasm of working with technology.
- There is need to develop a consistent conceptual framework for research in distance education.
- ICDE should promote research based on cooperation between institutions and organisations in different countries.

These recommendations hold good for Indian situation too.

Moore listed several areas of research for distance educators and institutions on the basis of the proceedings of the *Distance Education Research Symposium: A Research Agenda.* The research areas identified are:

- Research on policy and administration
- Research on instruction
- Research on Course Design
- Research on Learners and Learning

The suggested research agenda is applicable to Indian distance education field also.

17

Promotion and Coordination

The proposal to establish an Open University took concrete shape at a time when there was growing disenchantment with the ways in which the University and Higher Educations system had been developing in India. The system of Higher Education was already very large but its spread had been extremely uneven: the facilities available with individual universities varied widely, the courses offered by most universities had not been revised or renewed to meet the demand of the items, and therefore their relevance and utility were being questioned. The UGC which is responsible for development of universities was not able to do much as funding for higher education was continuously declining. It is against this background that the search for an alternative system for the provision of educational opportunities began and the decision to establish on Open University was taken, in 1985.

Towards the end of 1991, a consensus emerged among all the participating interests, for the establishment of a statutory mechanism under IGNOUAct to perform the function of promotion and coordination of the open university system in India. This mechanism, it was agreed, would be known as the Distance Education Council (DEC) which would function within the broad framework and the policies laid down by the Board of Management of IGNOU while enjoying a significant measure of autonomy in its operations. A statute was framed for establishing the DEC which became operational in February 1992.

Functions of the DEC

The DEC has been assigned the following powers and functions:

- promotion of the open university/ distance education system, its coordinated development, and the determination of its standards;
- development of a network of open universities/ distance education institutions in India;
- identification of priority areas in which distance education programmes should be organised, including the specific client groups and the types of programmes, and the provision of support for organising such programmes through a network;
- promotion of training programme for distance educators;

- initiating and organising measures for joint development of programmes and courses as well as research in distance education technology and practices;
- evolving the pattern and nature of development funding for open universities/ distance education institutions;
- establishing and developing arrangements for coordinating and sharing the instructional material prepared by different open universities/ distance education institutions as well as student support systems with a view to avoiding any duplication of efforts;
- evolving procedure for sharing courses and programmes and also laying down the terms and conditions for such sharing;
- collection, compilation and dissemination of information about courses and programmes offered by open universities and distance education institutions;
- periodic review of the performance of open universities/ distance education institutions participating in the network;
- preparation of guidelines for courses and programmes (content, structure and production) as well as for the delivery of various services to students;
- provision of funding for the development of open universities/ distance education institutions and the establishment of mechanisms for determining the extent and scope of such funding.

During the initial years, DEC took several measures to fulfill its mandate. DEC set up a Quality Assurance Panel, as a standing committee to advise the Council on all matters relating to the maintenance of quality in DE. Its terms of reference are:

- to recommend a set of measure that open universities should initiate to ensure an acceptable quality for distance education programmes.
- to formulate and recommend guidelines and procedure for programme identification and development, involving identification of learner groups, strategies and methods for course development and preparation, media-mix, delivery mechanisms, student assessment procedures, etc.
- to develop and recommend performance indicators for evaluation of ongoing programmes of distance education from the point of view of the quality of their processes and study materials.
- to recommend guideline for the exchange and sharing of instructional materials, including adoption, adaptation and translation and also the student support services.

- to recommend norms, procedures and practices in respect of admission, evaluation, completion of course requirements, and transfer of credits of students admitted to open university programmes.
- to undertake from time to time, studies on the implementation of quality assurance measures by the open universities and their impact on programmes with a view to evolving procedures for validation of programmes and their eventual accreditation.

Ministry of HRD in December 2012 issued certain directions with regard to regulations, maintenance of standards and according recognition to DE programmes conducted by higher education institutions. These are:

- UGC shall act as a regulator in respect of ODL programmes, and universities/ institutions need to seek recognition/ permission from UGC for conducting such programmes;
- UGC will develop regulations for maintenance of norms and standards in ODL programmes in accordance with the recommendation of the Madhav Menon Committee Report (December, 2011)
- UGC will create necessary physical infrastructure and manpower to discharge the regulatory functions and for the purpose utilise the staff of erstwhile DEC, in consultation with IGNOU
- UGC shall as a soon as DEC is dissolved start performing to functions as the regulator of ODL programmes.

N.R. Madhava Menon Committee Constituted by the UGC made the following recommendations:

"The need for an alternative strategy to supplement the conventional system of higher education has been appreciated and accepted long back by the policy makers of the country. Through various policy and programme interventions, attempts have been made to promote Open and Distance Learning (ODL) system to facilitate the expansion of higher education sector for the fulfillment of aspirations of those who are deprived of pursuing it for whatever reason. As a result, the contribution of ODL to Gross Enrollment Ratio (GER) in higher education has risen to about 22 per cent. But, a lot still remains to be done. With the increasing use of technology all over the world in providing learning support to ODL students, the Committee finds it appropriate to recommend well regulated expansion of ODL system in the higher education sector in the country during the 12th Plan period to help fulfill the aspirations of the seekers of knowledge and skill by enhancing the opportunities at affordable cost for the benefit of all those who have the desire to educate themselves further but cannot do so on a full time basis.

The Committee is very much concerned with the complaints about the quality of self learning materials used by a few ODL institutions, inadequate infrastructure facilities at headquarters and study centres, lack of proper student support services and delivery of programmes through franchisees leading to lowering of the overall quality of education and its commercialisation. This has shaken the faith of the employer groups and also common people in the ODL system.

In view of the above challenges, the Committee recommends establishment of an independent and effective Regulatory Authority on Distance Education, equipped with necessary powers and resources, through an Act of the Parliament to determine and regulate the standards of higher education including technical education through ODL and to promote and co-ordinate amongst the stake holders for dissemination of quality higher education relevant to the need of the individual and society. This independent Regulatory Authority may be called the Distance Education Council of India (DECI). Eventually when the NCHER bill is passed DECI will get subsumed into the proposed overarching Regulator along with other existing regulators, viz. UGC, AICTE, NCTE, etc.

The Committee is aware that passing of the proposed Distance Education Council of India Bill may take some time. Meanwhile, the existing ambiguity and uncertainty cannot be allowed to prevail and be exploited by the foul players of the ODL system. There is a moral dilemma before the DEC, a statutory body of an open university i.e. IGNOU, in acting as a regulator of the ODL system regulating other open universities. Before the commencement and even after some years of commencement of the IGNOU Act, the UGC remained the regulator in respect of distance education system. Therefore, position of UGC vis-a-vis IGNOU as a Regulator is stronger and more acceptable to the whole university system including the open universities.

Keeping all this in view, the Committee recommends that the Government should issue a policy direction/notification to UGC for assuming the responsibilities of maintaining standards in ODL System and creating a DECI like interim authority for the purpose. Needless to say that while doing so the UGC and the interim authority will utilise the framework and resources available with the DEC working under IGNOU."

Recognition of higher education institutions for DE programmes was explained by UGC in terms of the following heads:

1. Eligibility criteria and conditions for recognition.
2. Period of validity, renewal and withdrawal of recognition.
3. Self regulation through disclosures, declarations and reports.
4. Quality assurance.

5. Minimum standards to be maintained.
6. Self learning materials.
7. Use of technology.
8. Programme launching process and approval.
9. Student admissions.
10. Learner centres and learner support service.
11. Evaluation and certification.
12. System management.
13. Research programmes.
14. Assessment and accreditation.

In pursuance of the directions issued by the Ministry of Human Resource Development, Department of Higher Education, Government of India dated 29.12.2012, the regulatory functions with regard to Distance Education programmes in higher education got vested with the University Grants Commission. The Distance Education Council which was the erstwhile regulator of Distance Education programmes, is dissolved and all regulatory functions are undertaken by the UGC. The UGC is in the process of framing new Regulations for Distance Education. It has, however, been decided that till such time the new Regulations of the UGC are notified, the guidelines of the erstwhile DEC with regard to recognition of ODL institutions shall be implemented for the purposes of grant of permission to institutions for Distance Education programmes.

Distance Education Council of India

Subject to the provisions of the University Grants Commission Act, 1956 or The All India Council for Technical Education Act, 1987, Pharmacy Council of India, National Council for Teacher Education, Indian Council of Agricultural Research, Indian Nursing Council, Council of Architecture, Medical Council of India, Rehabilitation Council of India, Dental Council of India, Central Homeopathic Council and others, providing for the coordination, determination and regulation of standards in various fields of higher education, it shall be the duty of the Council to take necessary steps for the promotion, coordination and determination of standards of the distance education system relating to higher education and for that purpose, the Council may:

- lay down norms, guidelines and standards for offering various programmes of higher education through distance education system and prescribe physical and infrastructural facilities, staffing pattern and staff qualifications required for such programmes and enforce the same;

- grant recognition to programmes of higher education offered through distance education system within the country and/ or outside;
- act as a nodal authority for providing communication network tools, technologies, radio broadcast, telecast, internet, satellite communication and the interactive technology relevant for distance education;
- establish collaborative network of higher education institutions for joint development and/ or sharing of educational resources;
- establish and maintain centres or higher education institutions of distance education for providing common facilities and services, and for promotion of research, innovation and training for study learning material course writers, moderators and technical personnel working in ODL system;
- lay down norms, guidelines and standards for regulating and monitoring online programmes; regulate the collaboration between foreign education providers and Indian higher education institutions and take steps to prevent commercialisation of distance education system;
- assess the financial needs, allocate and disburse grants out of the Fund of the Council to a recognised higher education intuition offering programmes through distance mode for such purposes as may be prescribed by regulations;
- develop guidelines for charging fees by higher education institutions imparting distance education so that fee is commensurate and not exorbitant to recover the cost of development of the programme;
- advise the Central and State Governments, Union Territory Administrations, Universities and Open Universities, on the following matters on demand:
  a) establishment of new open universities and institutions of distance education;
  b) release of grants to higher education institutions of distance education for any general or specific purpose;
  c) selection of Vice-Chancellor for an open university;
  d) introduction of a programme through distance education in a university or an institution not having such system of education; and
  e) any other matter relating to distance education.
- undertake surveys and studies on matters related to distance education;

- prescribe norms and standards for appraisal of higher education institutions imparting distance education; coordinate with the University Grants Commission and other regulatory and promotional bodies in the field of higher education, for the fulfillment of the objective of this Act;
- undertake inspection of higher education institutions imparting distance education in the manner as may be laid down by regulations and issue necessary directives for removal of deficiencies, if any;
- take such measures as are necessary to maintain prescribed norms and standards in the higher education institutions offering distance education programmes including derecognition;
- to lay down criteria for equivalence of degree, diploma and certificate awarded through distance education system vis a vis conventional system;
- take all necessary steps to prevent commercialisation of open and distance education;
- perform such other functions as may be prescribed.

New Distance Education Council bill has not yet become law. There has been considerable delay in enacting the new law. Distance Education Bureau of UGC is supposed to perform the functions of the proposed DEC of India. This situation attracted criticism from many quarters. A former Pro-Vice chancellor of IGNOU remarked: "More than three years have passed and UGC has been managing the show without its heart into it. There is a lurking fear that the ODL system, which caters to millions of students from diverse backgrounds has been pushed into deep identity crisis. The ODL system is swimming against the tide and has been pushed on the verge of tsunami…."

18

Need for National Policy

Distance education is becoming an increasingly significant policy choice for developing countries. A policy is a written course of actions, such as statue, procedure and regulation. A distance education policy is a written course of action to facilitate the development of distance education.

The critical issues in policy and planning for distance education system are:

- Identifying the target population and their needs.
- Choosing the type of system.
- Choosing the appropriate technology of delivering.
- Business planning and costing distance education system.
- Materials developing.
- Tutoring and supporting students.
- Enrolling students.
- Assessing students.
- Managing and administrating the distance education system.
- Monitoring, evaluation and quality assurance.

This list indicates the areas of decision making and highlights the range of decisions policy makers and planners have to address in establishing and maintaining distance education systems.

Despite the practice of distance education for over half a century, India lacks a clear policy on the subject.

With the success of the University of Delhi correspondence courses in 1962, and later the first Open University in Andhra Pradesh in 1982, the Government of India established IGNOU in 1985 by an Act of Parliament, a landmark in the history of ODL in India as it gave IGNOU the dual rights to offer programmes as well as determine standards of teaching, evaluation and research in ODL. But, until the establishment of Distance Education Council in 1991, IGNOU could not put into practice the standard setting role in ODL. The New Education Policy of 1986 emphasised the role of IGNOU in spreading technical and management education. In 1995, the CABE committee on distance education recommended establishment of open university in each of Indian States. In the absence of written policy, the system has been used and abused over the years.

The recommendations of the National Knowledge Commission (NKC) established by the Government of India reflects the importance of ODL, as it called for radical reform of the system of open and distance education (ODE) to achieve the objectives of expansion, inclusion and excellence in higher education. While it recognised ODL as a discipline, it recommended several measures to improve the provision of ODL in India. Some of the recommendations (NKC, 2007) are:

- Create a national ICT infrastructure for networking ODE institutions.
- Set up a National Education Foundation to develop web-based common open resources.
- Establish a credit bank to effect transition to a course credit system.
- Establish a National Education Testing Service for assessing ODE students.
- Facilitate convergence with conventional universities.
- Set up a Research Foundation to support research activity in ODE.
- Overhaul training programmes for educators.
- Increase access for learners with special needs.
- Create a new Standing Committee for the regulation of ODE.
- Develop a system for quality assessment.

While some of the recommendations have been taken up by the Government of India to implement, it is important to note that the NKC indirectly questioned the quality of ODL, while recommending that graduates through ODL mode need to pass a national eligibility test apart from their university examination. Nevertheless, the NKC was concerned about the low Gross Enrollment Ratio (GER) in the country, and viewed ODL as a means to improve the same, but without compromising quality.

Draft National ODL Policy (2009)

The Government of India for the first time came out with a draft National Policy on ODL on 28 August 2009, and emphasised that while the danger of the large number of ODL providers turning into "degree mills" is higher, ODL has important roles to play: (i) that providing opportunity of learning to those, who do not have direct access to face to face teaching, working persons, home-makers, etc,; (ii) providing opportunity to working professionals to update their knowledge, enabling them to switchover to new disciplines and professions and enhancing their qualifications for career advancement; (iii) exploiting the potential of Information and Communication Technology (ICT) in the teaching and learning process; and (iv) achieving the target of 15 per cent of GER by the end of 11th Plan and 20 per cent by the end of 12th Five Year Plan.

The draft policy highlighted some positive, measures identified by the Government, while, it largely detailed out the rules for controlling ODL practices by providing a regulatory framework. However, it also identified some of the important policy directions:

- ODL to be regulated by the Standing Committee of the National Commission for Higher Education and Research (NCHER), when established;
- Programme approval to be made mandatory with penal provisions for violators;
- Franchising of ODL not to be permitted by any institution, whether public or private;
- Offer of programmes through distance mode should be allowed for which there are required departments and faculties prior to offer of the programmes;
- Mandatory use of ICTs to delivery programmes and management of the student and university affairs;
- Optimal use of e learning contents for delivery/ offering their programmes through distance and enable student-teacher and student-student interaction;
- Distance education shall focus on providing opportunity of education to people at educationally disadvantaged situations such as living in remote and rural areas, adults with no or limited access to education of their choice, etc;
- Establishment of a credit bank and credit transfer system;
- Convergence of the face to face mode teaching departments of conventional universities with their distance education directorates/ correspondence course wings to bridge gaps, if any;
- Reputed foreign education providers to offer programmes subject to fulfilling of legal requirements;
- Creation of favourable environment for research on ODL;
- Encourage training and orientation for teachers and administrators of ODL system;
- Create national ICT infrastructure for ODL; and
- Provide educational opportunities for learners with disabilities and senior citizens.

While the regulatory provisions mentioned within the draft ODL policy (2009) were in detail, and some of those were controversial, the above policy directions identified were very positive. However, after the initial discussions, the policy could not be finalised.

Need for National ODL Policy

The National ODL policy should be comprehensive and forward looking. It should help UGC and other regulatory agencies in understanding and appreciating the role of ODL in the overall educational scene of the country. In the words of Sanjay Mishra, the policy should answer the following questions:

- What should be the policy to provide access to quality education for all?
- Can we depend only on face-to-face education to provide access to learning opportunities to all at a time when citizens need regular up-gradation of skills and knowledge?
- Should institutions consider ODL/ Learning as cash cow?
- What are the responsibilities of educational institutions?
- What would enable institutions to create systems and processes to improve quality?
- Should ODL be treated as a "degree mill", and why not?
- What are the responsibilities of the leaner and educational providers in ODL?

The policy should have the following three objectives:

- to provide increased access to quality educational opportunities in all domains of knowledge,
- to provide increased freedoms to the learners in terms of their choice of courses, place of study, time of study,
- to provide lifelong learning opportunities to working people, and those who have interest to learn.

Sanjay Mishra suggested the following structural framework for ODL policy.

Suggested Focus Areas for ODL Policy

Key ODL Policy Area	*Descriptions*
Definitions	Provides explanatory notes on terms used such as ODL, open education, OER, access, equity, quality, continuous assessment, term end assessment, learner support, self-learning materials, e Learning, etc.
Curriculum Design and Development	Statutory compliance of course design and development, need based programmes, credit transfer, admission criteria, accreditation of courses, nature of learning materials, media-mix, technology integration, adherence to academic calendar, etc.

Governance/ Administration/ Financial	Institutional mechanisms to grievance redressal, cost of tution, charging overhead cost, profit from ODL, principles of budgeting, adherence to national accounting practices, fee reimbursement and distribution of bursaries, staffing, monitoring and evaluation, internal quality assurance, etc.
Staff Development and Research	Workload , staff training, performance appraisal, encouragement for research on ODL, publication of research output on institutional repository, etc.
Legal	Issues related to compliance with national policy on education, equivalence and parity of courses and programmes, use of OER, etc.
Learner Support and Assessment	Responsibilities of the learners, counselling, tutoring, continuous assessment, library access, laboratory provisions, partnership with other organisations for services, use of media for support, proctorial nature of term end evaluation, grading, etc.
Technical/ Infrastructural	Provisions of technical support, call centre, hardware and software issues, use of open source and open format, accountability of performance of the systems, etc.

(Adapted from: King et al, 2000)

19

Weaknesses and Deficiencies of Distance Education System

In spite of its several accomplishments, the distance education system in India exhibits the following major weaknesses and deficiencies:

- Distance education system is thinly spread.
- Spread of distance learners is uneven.
- Distance courses by and large are liberal and general in nature.
- Professional, vocational and technical courses are a few and are limited to Diploma and Certificates levels.
- Majority of distance learners are men.
- Learning materials are not fully self instructional.
- Distance teaching is mostly print based and not multimedia based.
- Student support services are inadequate, insufficient and uneven.
- In many institutions sufficient academic staff is absent.
- Staff training activities are very limited. Most of the course writers, tutors, counsellors, coordinators, and producers remain untrained and unoriented.
- Organisational structures are not on sound and established principles. Systems are centralised.
- More than one institution run identical courses thereby duplicating efforts resulting in low enrollments in many places.
- Study Centres are mostly concentrated in urban areas.
- Not much attention is paid to feedback mechanisms; assignments are not evaluated and returned to the students in time wherever they are.
- Student contact programmes and tutorial services are not many.
- Considerable delay occurs in the dispatch of course materials to the students.
- Laboratory and library facilities are not adequate and wherever they exist they are much below the standards.
- Efforts are not made to evaluate and check the standards of the system. Its growth and working is haphazard leaving much to be desired.
- Apex organisation to monitor the maintenance of standards in institutions and to coordinate the activities is absent.

- Research on the system is qualitatively and quantitatively limited and poor. Most of it is informative and descriptive and fails to give new directions.

Commissions, Committees, Working Groups, Task Forces, Study Teams, Evaluation Reports, Research Studies, Observations and Comments of Distance Education Experts, etc. pointed out the above mentioned weaknesses and shortcomings.

Correspondence Institutes of Conventional Universities

Majority of distance courses are provided by Correspondence Courses institutes (some of which are recently re-designated as Centres of Distance Education) of conventional universities which do not enjoy independence, autonomy and freedom to experiment and innovate. Correspondence Courses institutes have inbuilt resistance to changes and are sensitive to the new educational demands. Committees, studies and research investigations from time to time identified several weaknesses in these institutes. Some of such weaknesses and deficiencies are:

1. Most of the Correspondence institutes do not have competent and adequate staff. Best teachers are not posted to work in these institutes and as a result they have low motivation.
2. More than one university in a state started correspondence courses thereby duplicating efforts resulting in low enrollments in many places.
3. Lessons are prepared in a hurry with no regard to quality.
4. Not much attention is paid to the assignments; they are not evaluated, corrected and returned to the students in time.
5. Most of the correspondence courses do not have study centres and personal contact programmes are organised by only a few institutions.
6. Too much reliance is placed on the printed material and latest communication technology is hardly made use of.
7. There is considerable delay in the dispatch of course material to the students.
8. Bodies charged with the running of these institutions are not organised properly.
9. The system has the same rigidities in the courses offered as the formal system; the students offer the same courses and appear for the same examinations as the regular students.
10. Rarely laboratory and library facilities are provided and where they exist are much below the standards.
11. They do not have identity of their own as they work within the university structure. The latter pay perfunctory attention to the former.
12. Rarely efforts are made to evaluate and check the standards of those correspondence courses. Therefore, their growth and working is haphazard leaving much to be desired.

The open universities when compared to correspondence institutes are definitely better in organisational structure and performance but much desires to be done in achieving the objectives of distance higher education.

Distance education potential is increasingly recognised, but its expansion has not been significant. New Education Policy (1986) and its Programme of Action (1992) adopted by the Government of India recommended the establishment of an open university in each State during the Eighth Five Year Plan. It was further said that the "expansion in higher education has to be accommodated in an equitable and cost-effective manner, mainly by large scale expansion of the distance education system and by providing opportunities to large segments of population, particularly the disadvantaged groups, women and people living in backward and hilly areas". This did not happen. Correspondence institutes of conventional have very low enrollment. In addition to low spread, considerable variance occurs in the provision of distance education. No uniform pattern is visible among correspondence institutes. Admission procedures, eligibility criteria, course offering, student support systems, evaluation patterns differ from institute to institute. UGC has considered ways and means to systematise and expand the correspondence courses and to upgrade them to real distance mode, but its efforts have not yet yielded fruits.

How to Improve?

How to improve the scene of distance education? Sometime back this question was debated and discussed by (1) the University Grants Commission which is responsible for the promotion of distance education in conventional universities, (2) the Distance Education Council of Indira Gandhi National Open University whose objective is to coordinate, promote and maintain standards of distance education in all distance educational institutes, (3) the Central Advisory Board of Education of the Government of India, at the Round Table Conference on Quality Assurance in Distance Education Jointly organised by the Commonwealth of Learning, the University Grants Commission and the Distance Education Council, an Action Plan for immediate implementation was evolved. The Action Plan indicated the main responsibilities of the conventional universities, the correspondence institutes and the apex agencies. The Action Plan broadly was as follows:

Responsibility of the Universities

- Universities concerned will appoint Advisory Committees for the distance education units as recommended by the UGC.
- Universities concerned will develop detailed job descriptions specifying the academic, administrative and financial duties and the powers of the heads of the distance education units.

- Universities concerned will develop plans to ensure mobility of students from the distance stream to the conventional stream and vice versa.
- Universities will prepare plans for conducting training programmes, transforming materials, developing training materials.
- Universities will actively encourage the staff of the distance education units to take training in distance education activities.
- Universities will explore the feasibility of converting some portion of the degree requirements to the distance mode and make it possible for students to combine the distance and the face to face components.
- Universities will make plans to computerise certain essential operations of the distance education units.
- Each distance education unit will establish a mechanism for the systematic dissemination of information about its programmes.
- Soon each of the participating CCIs will identify and include in their instructional package at least 25 videos made by the UGC's country-wide Classroom Project.
- Soon each of the participating CCIs will develop detailed curriculums for at least two innovative and/ or employment/ skills oriented programmes/ courses.

Responsibility of the Apex Bodies

- To develop norms regarding the physical facilities.
- To make resources available for training.
- To initiate innovations regarding course structure: e.g., to explore the feasibility of combining the face to face and distance components in a single programme.
- To initiate the sharing of the resources of the audio-visual production facilities in the EMRC's and the AVRC's.
- To develop a policy regarding accreditation procedures.
- Development of a strategy to disseminate the Quality Assurance culture.

Nothing significant has happened since the Action Plan was drawn.

Essential Elements of Distance Education

The feasibility, appropriateness and utility of distance education in any country depends on its socio-economic-politico culture. The physical and human resources which exist in advanced and industrialised countries are not available in developing countries and this affects the operation of a distance teaching-learning system. Obviously the system of distance education has to suit the context. Even countries with similar levels of growth would differ according to geography, infrastructure, educational structure and quality and quantity of human resources. However, there are a core set of activities which need to work if a distance education system is to be effective operationally. Distance teaching institutes must:

- provide all learners with specially designed self-instructional learning materials in time.
- provide learners with opportunities for interaction with distance teachers and co-learners in a variety of ways.
- give learners feedback on their learning as rapidly as possible.
- maintain records processed within a given time-scale and used to manage the system.
- monitor key operational dimensions at the centre and in the field on a regular basis, using the data to help evaluation and improvement.
- monitor student progress continuously for individuals and groups, and modify materials and the system in response to findings.
- provide staff development and support to local support staff.
- Co-ordinate the functioning of the sub-systems in the whole operation (production of materials or programme support services, administrative functions and assessment activities) so that conditions conducive for learning exist for the learners.
- enable learners to complete courses successfully, with results comparable to reputed conventional systems, or with demonstrable skills;
- provide credible qualifications or accreditation where relevant.

Need for National Concern

For any national distance education system to be effective and efficient, certain conditions are essential, some of such are:

- Ruling parties' and groups' will.
- Support of political parties and social groups for educational modernisation and democratisation.
- Sensitivity of educational planners and administrators to the demands of educationally disadvantaged groups.
- Quest for educational experiments, innovations and reforms.
- Attitudinal change in the academics in conventional system of education.
- Strong belief that education can also be imparted by modes other than face-to-face.
- Recognition of the educational value and potential of emerging communication and information technologies.

20

Regulating Standards

Ministry of HRD, Government of India, appointed the Committee to suggest measures to regulate distance education in 2010, under the Chairmanship of N. R. Madhava Menon. The terms of reference of the Committee were:

- To harmonise the legal position in respect of distance education programmes in various disciplines, as they concern the UGC Act, AICTE Act and IGNOU Act
- To recommend framework for approval of Distance Education courses/institutions within functional jurisdiction of UGC, AICTE and DEC in dealing with the subject matters of distance education
- To recommend outcome benchmarks for distance education systems which will facilitate equivalence with conventional modes
- To recommended guideline for processing of the approval of technical programmes through distance and mixed mode
- To suggest ways towards enhanced contribution of Distance Education to reach the targeted Gross Enrollment Ratio (GER) of 30 per cent by 2020

Eight groups were constituted to deliberate separately and simultaneously on eight different contemporary and burning topics. Recommendations of all eight groups were discussed in the plenary session and finalised. Financial recommendations are given below.

Recommendations

Perspective

Higher Education sector has grown significantly in scale and size but it is still unable to meet the growing demands for it because of many reasons including resource constraints. It is not possible to meet this rising demand through the Capital-intensive conventional system of education only. The need for an alternative strategy to supplement the conventional system of higher education has been appreciated and accepted long back by the policy makers of the country. Through various policy and programme interventions, attempts have been made to promote Open and Distance Learning (ODL) system to facilitate the expansion of higher education sector for the fulfillment of aspirations of those who are deprived of pursuing it for whatever reason. As a result, the contribution of ODL to Gross Enrollment Ratio (GER) in higher education has risen to about 22 per cent. But, a lot still remains to be done. With the increasing use of technology all over the world in providing learning support to ODL students, the Committee finds it appropriate to recommend well regulated expansion of ODL system in the higher education sector in the country during the 12th Plan period to help fulfill the aspirations of the seekers of knowledge and skill by enhancing the opportunities at affordable cost for the benefit of all those who have the desire to educate themselves further but cannot do so on a full time basis.

Goal and Concerns for Quality

The Ministry of Human Resource Development has set a goal to achieve 30 per cent GER in higher education by the year 2020. As per the preliminary estimate prepared by the NUEPA, it would require an investment of about Rs. 9.5 lakh crores. The Committee is aware of the fact that the physical infrastructure created for imparting conventional education largely remains idle after the official working hours. Keeping this infrastructure idle and going for establishing new ones in conventional mode, firstly, would be a difficult proposition due to lack of resources and secondly, it would also tantamount to avoidable wastage of scarce national resources. AICTE has recently made provision for allowing second shift programmes at the graduate, post graduate and vocational and technical education through its approved institutions. The Committee recommends that every conventional university and institution, including technical and professional ones, should be encouraged to switch over to a dual mode of imparting education by offering ODL programmes in additional to the conventional programmes so that the already available infrastructure can be used as study centres for holding counselling and practical instruction not only on holidays but on every day after the working hours. This will automatically increase the enrollment by 2-3 times. Starting ODL programme would require preparation of appropriate study material and appointment of coordinators and counsellors in appropriate numbers. A centrally sponsored scheme should be devised by the Distance Education Council (DEC) to share the cost involved to encourage the conventional universities and institutions to start ODL programmes without delay.

The Committee is convinced that "Higher Education" means only and only "Quality Education", otherwise it loses its purpose and value. Eyebrows are often raised about the poor quality of education being imparted through ODL system, particularly, in respect of technical and professional programmes, which require development of certain skills through hands on practice. Presently, AICTE permits only MBA and MCA courses, that too, only if the Tripartite Committee (AICTE, UGC and DEC) approves them. The decision not to permit other technical and professional courses through distance mode is mainly due to their concern for quality. The committee, after having heard all point of views on the matter, is of the opinion that quality is not a matter of concern in ODL system only. It is a matter of equal concern in conventional system as well, whether it is general, technical or professional programmes.

The Committee, therefore, feels that barring technical and professional programmes totally through distance mode will be against the accepted policy of Government of India of expanding opportunities for higher education and making it inclusive as an instrument of democratising education and making it a lifelong process. The inherent advantages of the flexibility to move from education to work and vice versa and innovativeness of the ODL system, so well suited to the diverse requirements of the citizens of the country, need to be harnessed in full for enhancing the productivity of the human resource.

Besides, Part VI of the National Policy on Education 1986 dealing with "Technical and Management Education" stipulates in para 6.6 in unequivocal terms that "in view of the present rigid entry requirements to formal courses restricting the access of a large segment of people to technical and managerial (sic. management) education, programmes through a distance-learning process, including use of the mass media, will be offered. Technical and management education programmes, including education in polytechnics, will also be on a flexible modular pattern based on credits, with provision for multi-point entry. A strong guidance and counselling service will be provided."

The Committee is very much concerned with the complaints about the quality of self-learning materials used by a few ODL institutions, inadequate infrastructure facilities at headquarters and study centres, lack of proper student support services and delivery of programmes through franchisee leading to lowering of the overall quality of education and its commercialisation. This has shaken the faith of the employer groups and also common people in the ODL system. The Committee is also aware of the limitations of the UGC or DEC or AICTE or NCTE, in terms of necessary manpower and effective legal framework to reign in the foul players.

The Committee is, therefore, of the view that an effective regulatory system must be put in place before letting technical education through ODL mode is allowed extensively in all types of institutions. Before allowing technical and professional programmes through the ODL system, the DEC, in conformity with the AICTE norms and standards, will have to develop programme specific benchmarks, inter alia, for theory, tutorial/ counselling and practical, infrastructure and manpower requirement. Once such system is in position, the DEC should open the ODL system to technical and professional programmes gradually to the extent it can monitor and supervise effectively, either through inspections or technological interventions, to ensure that the learner acquires necessary skill before the completion of the programme.

Need for a New Legal Frame Work and ICT support

The UGC Act, 1956 provides for the co-ordination and determination of standards in university system by the UGC. Initially, when the correspondence course started there was no regulatory framework outside the university system. The statutory bodies of the respective universities devised the institutional arrangements and delivery mechanisms. Later on, when the number of universities offering correspondence courses started increasing, the University Grants

Commission, with a view to maintaining standards in distance education programmes, stepped in to issue Guidelines, Rules and Regulations from time to time. Till the enactment of the Indira Gandhi National Open University (IGNOU) Act, 1985, the UGC was the sole Regulator for the whole higher education system including the technical and distance education.

The provisions of the IGNOU Act suggest that the Parliament intended, for the purpose of regulatory arrangements, to treat higher education through open and distance learning differently from the conventional university system, in view of its unique characteristics. Therefore, while setting up a separate university, IGNOU, for imparting higher education through ODL system, the Act also gave the responsibility of development, coordination and determination of standards in the Open and Distance Education system to it, "notwithstanding anything contained in any other law for the time being in force". Accordingly, the IGNOU established the Distance Education Council in the year 1991 to discharge the responsibilities as a Regulator of the ODL system. It may be mentioned that unlike the UGC or the AICTE, the DEC is not a statutory body and thus does not enjoy powers to compel obedience to its regulations.

In 1987 the Government of India, by an Act of Parliament, established the All India Council for Technical Education (AICTE) with a view to ensuring proper planning and coordinated development of the technical education system throughout the country and the regulation and proper maintenance of norms and standards in the technical education system. The AICTE Act does not specifically provide for distance education programmes. The AICTE Act significantly excludes universities from its jurisdiction, but it gives the AICTE the authority to enforce the quality parameters of technical education in these universities. Therefore, it is only reasonable to infer that the AICTE has the mandate to maintain the norms and standards in technical education through the ODL system. Gazette notification No. 44, F. No.18_15/93-TD. V/TS.IV dated 1st March 1995 of Ministry of Human Resource Development, Government of India also supports this interpretation while providing that the degrees awarded through Distance

Education by the universities and institutions of national importance stand automatically recognised for the purpose of employment under the Central Government, provided it has been approved by DEC and wherever necessary by AICTE. In fact, this notification has necessitated the approval of the DEC for offering any ODL programme.

In order to streamline the process of recognition as a single window system and to avoid the duplication of efforts by the three Regulators (UGC, AICTE and DEC) in respect of ODL programmes, DEC constituted a Joint Committee of the three bodies through an MOU. However, the MOU could not become fully operational, much less effective, due to lack of coordination among them. In order to facilitate better coordination, a Tripartite Committee of the Chairpersons of the UGC, AICTE and DEC was constituted by the MHRD in the year 2010. This, too, does not seem to have delivered the desired results. Teacher Education programmes in distance mode also face almost similar problems and fate. The DEC has developed some norms and guidelines for offering programmes through distance mode. However, enforcing these norms and procedures remains a big challenge for them due to lack of adequate manpower and technological support. The resulting situation, in effect, leaves the field unregulated at least in some sectors.

In order to keep pace with the growing demand for recognition of ODL programmes, the DEC in the year 2007, decided to accord institutional recognition instead of programme specific recognition on the assumption that the appropriate academic bodies of universities/ institutions would take care of the quality of education imparted. Its orders do not indicate whether a university/ institution having recognition of the DEC for ODL courses, would require the approval of the AICTE for offering technical courses. On the basis of approval of DEC, many universities/ institutions started technical education programmes without the approval of the AICTE. A large number of them "misused" the opportunity for commercialisation of ODL system through unregulated expansion disregarding standards of education. The proliferation of such ODL institutions, behaving like degree dispensing mills, has affected the credibility and acceptability of such programmes adversely. As a result, many employers have refused to treat ODL degrees at par with the regular conventional degrees. A statutory body like the Bar Council of India has gone to the extent of disapproving the First Degree obtained through ODL for eligibility to join the professional law course. In 2009, vide D.O. No. 6-7/2009-DL, the Government of India directed the DEC to immediately withdraw permission given to various institutions to conduct B.Tech/ BE programmes through distance mode and ensure that no student is admitted further in these courses. In spite of DEC's order to stop the B.Tech/ BE courses and AICTE's repeated advertisements in the newspapers about non-recognition of these courses, it is reported that such courses are continuing to be offered by many institutions. It is interesting to note that there is no legal provision to take such institutions to task who offer ODL courses without recognition from the DEC. Even statutory regulators like UGC, AICTE and NCTE have not been able to take effective action against fake universities institutions offering courses in contravention of the relevant Acts.

The Committee is of the view that inadequacy and ambiguity in the legal framework and inability of DEC to discipline erring institutions are the main reasons for lack of regulation in the ODL system resulting in some cases in poor quality of education. The Committee is aware that the enactment of the Prohibition of Unfair Practices in Technical Educational Institutions, Medical Educational Institutions and Universities Bill, 2010, the National Accreditation Regulatory Authority for Higher Educational Institutions Bill, 2010 and the proposed National Council for Higher Education and Research Bill will address all the above issues faced by the Higher Education System generally and technical and professional education in particular. There are some other immediate pressing issues affecting the regulation of ODL system adversely, viz., the propriety of one open university (IGNOU) controlling the standards of other open universities through statute created by itself, the legality of State Open Universities offering ODL courses outside the State territory, the legality of franchising of education etc., which can be resolved only through a Parliamentary intervention.

In view of the above challenges, the Committee recommends to establish an independent and effective Regulatory Authority on Distance Education, equipped with necessary powers and resources, through an Act of the Parliament to determine and regulate the standards of higher education including technical education through ODL and to promote and coordinate amongst the stakeholders for dissemination of quality higher education relevant to the need of the individual and society. This independent Regulatory Authority may be called the Distance Education Council of India (DECI). Eventually, when the NCHER Bill is passed, DECI will get subsumed into the proposed overarching Regulator along with other existing regulators, viz. UGC, AICTE, NCTE, etc.

A draft Distance Education Council Bill for the establishment of an independent Regulatory Authority is enclosed with this Report. This enactment would simultaneously require the following amendments in the IGNOU Act, 1985 also:

i. Deletion of "and for the coordination and determination of standards in such system" from the preamble of the Act.
ii. Deletion of "and to coordinate and determine the standards of such system" from Section 4 of the Act.
iii. Deletion of Section 5 (2) of the Act.
iv. Deletion of Section 24 (i) of the Act.
v. Deletion of "and the Distance Education Council from Statute 2 (1) and substitution of," after the word "Board" by "and"; and
vi. Deletion of Statute 28 relating to the Distance Education Council.

In order to avoid any confusion arising out of the multiplicity of command, the Committee recommends that DECI should have the sole responsibility to recognise the distance education programmes, including technical and professional ones. Use of ICT for developing a web-based repository of high quality self-learning material and other aspects leading to maintenance of quality in the ODL system needs to be built into the said system by appropriate legal framework.

Quality Benchmarks

It will be the duty of the proposed DECI to ensure that the nomenclature of the degrees proposed to be awarded through such programmes are approved by the UGC, the institute has the requisite recognition from the respective regulatory authorities, viz., AICTE, MCI, DCI, etc. for the regular course in conventional mode, it is affiliated to a university, it has developed the self learning material of desired standards, it has a credible system of counselling, evaluation of assignments and examination, it has the necessary infrastructure including laboratories, library, class rooms, etc. and qualified counsellors as per the relevant norms. No conditional or post facto recognition shall be granted by the DECI. While granting recognition for Diploma and Certificate courses, the DECI must also ensure that the programme content in terms of both, theory as well as practical, are in consonance with the standards of such courses offered by various State Technical Education Boards, etc. so that credit transferability and flexibility of exit and re-entry are facilitated. Flexibility in learning and quality of learning have to go hand in hand to make the ODL programme acceptable to institutions admitting such learners to a higher education programme or the employer recruiting the graduates as the case may be.

Easily accessible high quality self-learning material and vibrant study centres are the two measurable elements of successful ODL institutions. Conventional system of maintenance of quality through expert inspections is not feasible. A national ICT backbone would enhance access and c-governance in ODL system and enable interactive learning and dissemination of knowledge through all modes i.e. print, audio-visual and internet based multimedia. DECI should collaborate with the National Mission on Education through ICT to avail the web-based high quality educational resources being developed by it. It should also endeavour to develop a sharable pool of self-learning material.

ODL in Conventional Universities

A conventional university/ institution will be granted recognition by DECI only for such ODL programmes, which are being offered through the regular conventional mode, and the syllabus and the evaluation for the award of the degree/ diploma shall be common for both, the conventional and the distance mode. This does not mean that specialised self learning material, counselling classes, submission of requisite number of assignments by the distance learner and their timely evaluation by the university will be compromised in any manner. In order to discourage commercialisation of distance education programmes, the Committee recommends that if the ODL prograrmne is offered through study centres, then the institution will have to restrict its study centres within the statutory territorial jurisdiction of the relevant Act/ Statutes governing it. The study centres should essentially have the necessary infrastructure and other facilities prescribed by the DECI. Franchising of study centres in private unrecognised colleges or organisations shall not be permitted. The State private universities may also be treated alike.

ODL in Open Universities

The Open Universities can be granted recognition for offering general, technical or professional degree programmes from its campus and study centres having necessary infrastructure and other facilities prescribed by the DECI. Before granting recognition, the DECI will ensure, inter alia, that the syllabi of various courses of open universities are not inferior to the model syllabi of the UGC in respect of general courses, AICTE in respect of technical and professional courses and of the respective Boards in respect of diploma courses and there is a credible system of evaluating the theoretical and practical attainments of the learner. UGC's decision not to permit Ph.D programme through distance education mode may be reviewed in the light of the National Policy on Education. However, the concern for quality behind such ban has to be addressed through a comprehensive and effective regulating mechanism and not by banning ODL mode for the degree.

ODL in Institutions Deemed to be Universities

UGC's decision not to allow institutions deemed to be universities to offer distance education programmes at all needs to be reviewed in the light of the National Policy on Education. However, the concern for quality behind such ban may be addressed through a comprehensive and effective regulation. An institution deemed to be a university established before the UGC Regulations, 2010 will be granted recognition by DECI only for such ODL programmes, which are being offered through the regular conventional mode, and the syllabus and the examination shall be common for both, the conventional and the distance mode. UGC Regulations, 2010 do not permit affiliation of colleges by deemed universities. The Committee recommends that the same principle may be applied for the opening of the study centres by the deemed universities as well, meaning thereby that these deemed universities may be allowed to operate study centres from their main and satellite campuses only, but not through affiliated colleges of other universities or franchisee centres.

Online ODL

With the advancement of technology, the concept of territorial jurisdiction of the institution offering higher education through ODL system has become irrelevant, but the Committee is also conscious of the fact that in past, several institutions have franchised the delivery of programmes to many undeserving individuals/ organisations, such practice with commercial motives has degenerated the teaching learning process to mere degree dispensing exercise. Therefore, the Committee recommends that if all the components, viz. admission, Learning Management System (LMS), counselling, submission of assignment and evaluation and final examination of the ODL programme are offered completely online, then there will be no restriction on territorial limits. For offering such online programmes, however, the universities including institutions deemed to be universities and other institutions will have to obtain prior approval of the DECI.

Equivalence of Degree

As the syllabi and the examination are common for the conventional as well as the ODL system in the dual mode institutions and the syllabi of the open universities are to be in consonance with the model curriculum of UGC/ AICTE etc., the Committee recommends that the degree imparted through the ODL system should be treated at par with the conventional system both for education as well as employment purposes. However, for the purpose of record, the degree/ certificate of the ODL learner should mention "through Distance Mode" or "through online" as the case may be on its face.

Interim Arrangement

The Committee is aware that passing of the proposed Distance Education Council of India Bill may take some time. Meanwhile, the existing ambiguity and uncertainty cannot be allowed to prevail and be exploited by the foul players of the ODL system. There is a moral dilemma before the DEC, a statutory body of an open university i.e. IGNOU, in acting as a regulator of the ODL system regulating other open universities. Before the commencement and even after some years of commencement of the IGNOU Act, the UGC remained the regulator in respect of distance education system. Therefore, position of UGC vis-a-vis IGNOU as a regulator is stronger and more acceptable to the whole university system including the open universities. Keeping all this in view, the Committee recommends that the Government should issue a policy direction/ notification to UGC for assuming the responsibilities of maintaining standards in ODL System and creating a DECI like interim authority for the purpose. Needless to say that while doing so the UGC and the interim authority will utilise the framework and resources available with the DEC working under IGNOU. First of all the interim authority shall evolve systems taking into account the observations made in this report, viz. development of programme specific quality benchmarks in respect of all relevant parameters, system for online application and processing, and disclosure of relevant information on the website of the institution and the DECI, development of quality self learning material, credible system of counselling, evaluation of assignments and examination, etc. Once the systems are in position, the DECI of UGC may start the recognition of ODL institutions as per the newly developed system and enforce norms and standards laid by it in the recognised institutions.

21

Status of Indian State Open Universities

Commonwealth Educational Media Centre for Asia (CEMCA) of Commonwealth of Learning (COL) in 2015 published a Report on the Status of State Open Universities in India. This Report on the Status of State Open Universities in India provides an overview of the growth of open education. It critically examines the recognition of qualifications, standards and regulations and the preparedness of ODL in India for the 21st century. The Report makes recommendations which will provide concrete guidelines for policy makers, administrators and other stakeholders in dealing with the issues and concerns facing ODL in the country.

The Report first described the following dimensions of open universities:

- Mission and Mandate
- Learner Enrollment
- Types of Programmes
- Pattern of Enrollment
- Profile of Learners
- Learners Success
- Pedagogy and Technology in Pedagogy
- Learner Support
- Learner Evaluation
- Income and Expenditure

The distinct issues from the scenario presented in the first part are outlined and discussed in sections: 1) Recognition of Awards, 2) Standards and Regulations, and 3) Preparedness for the 21st century. In the third section, 16 aspects are discussed.

The final section concluded with remarks and recommendations.

Key Recommendations

The discussions in the Report led to the following recommendations.

1. *The Projection and the Objective*: If India wants to benefit from her demographic dividend, and become a global production hub, she needs 500 million people with market-relevant skills by the middle of the 2020. The conventional universities, with the limitations

of their concrete walls and those of the voice of a teacher in the classroom, can serve the purpose, but only in a limited way. Given the possibilities which their pedagogies can materialise, the OUs are well placed to help in achieving this objective. To do so successfully, they should get together and form a National Forum of the OUs to engage in purposeful deliberations so as to collectively plan and devise strategies for: i) undoing the existing legal dampers they are faced with, ii) harnessing and utilising ICTs to their fullest potential cost-effectively, ii) sharing their resources (material, spatial and human) and research outcomes on a regular basis, and iv) working together towards building a learning society that is enabled to work for our economic growth and global security.

2. *New Target Groups and Certification of Previous Learning*: In order to materialise Recommendation 1, the OUs have to extend their reach to new target groups, apart from the New Learner — the target group that became the focus of ODL operations in the mid-1980s. There are other groups that have remained ignored so far, though they contribute to national economy in their own meagre ways. A significant proportion of these groups are the workers who work in the unorganised sector. Unlike here in India, a carpenter, a mason or a nanny in the USA has to have an appropriate license to practice their trade or profession. Such licenses are obtained formally after one displays the requisite knowledge and expertise in one's field and also satisfactory knowledge and understanding of the federal and the State laws/ regulations pertaining to one's trade/ profession. It is time that the OUs in India extended their efforts to such workers too, partly to improve their know-how to make them more productive and partly to open the gates for their growth along the mainstream of education. To materialise this possibility, it is necessary to: i) develop approaches and mechanisms to certify previous learning of all sorts including the skills, various competencies, arts and crafts passed on from generation to generation within families, and also ii) work out equivalences of the credentials gained by such worker-learners with those available in mainstream systems, so as to allow credit transfers across the diverse learning domains. This would open new horizons of growth and development as a consequence of satisfactory engagements, which in turn would contribute not only to a better quality of life and economic growth, but also to national and international security and peace.

3. *New Approaches Pedagogy*: Given the myriad levels and characteristics of the new learner as well as the sought after new learner groups-workers of all kinds in the unorganised sector, craftsmen/ women, those engaged in family trades or crafts, digital illiterates, digital immigrants and digital natives together with the qualified (in the conventional sense) university entrants at different levels, the dynamic institutions of higher education have to adopt unconventional pedagogical approaches to meet the challenge of imparting education to such a diverse and dispersed clientele. We have to evolve a pedagogical approach that provides the country with the means to cover the unreached; deliver education and training in all the known fields of human endeavour (languages, philosophy, liberal arts, humanities, sciences, technology, medicine, productive skills and competencies) at all the known levels; provide study and training material, learning experiences and teaching learning transactions in different formats, in different ways on different occasions on demand. If this sounds Utopian it would help to recall the pedagogical approach, namely transmodal education/ pedagogy[3], adopted by the University of Southern Queensland, Australia, to cater to its diverse learner populations dispersed nationally as well as internationally. To materialise Recommendations 1 and 2, the Indian OUs need to revisit their approaches to pedagogy. Many aspects of transmodal pedagogy are promising and relevant to our needs, provided its prerequisites are appreciated and put in place before taking the plunge.

Talking of the prerequisites, pedagogy, (transmodal or otherwise) hinges on: i) the content and skill or competencies to be imparted and learnt, and ii) the form they are put in for presentation to learners. The first of these points to 'curricula' (*see* Recommendation 4) and the second to 'technology'.

4. *New Approaches to Curricula, Instructional Design and Support Services*: Considering our educational objectives (*see* Recommendation 1) and the diverse target groups (*see* Recommendation 2), we are in dire need of: i) filling the knowledge and skill gaps in bulk of our education in general and the technical education in particular, ii) providing market-oriented and industry-integrated courses/ programmes, iii) satisfying the rising demand for "learning on demand" and work-integrated learning, and iv) merging and mixing the conventionally distinct disciplines, across their lines of distinction, giving credence to new branches of learning. To satisfy these needs, it is not just desirable, but crucially necessary to develop: i) new curricula that are socio-economically relevant, ii) new approaches to instructional design for some of such curricula and the courses they lead to, one may visualise, classroom teaching could be their undoing. Such new learner-centered curricula and the related innovative instructional design alone will not serve the desired purpose, unless they are strongly supported by flawless learner support services twenty-four seven. Positive efforts on the suggested lines alone can ensure India's position as a *production hub* in the next few decades. And the OUs, free as they are from the legacy curricula and the related staff and structures, are well placed to meet this challenge.

5. *Extensive use of ICTs*: In pursuit of the contemporary technology driven reformative agenda, one cannot but take recourse to the extensive use of ICTs in order to materialise Recommendations 1 and 2. Again, their use is at the very core of Recommendations 3 and 4 as well. To make any headway in the process of achieving our objectives, in line with the strategies proposed above, the only option we have is to harness ICTs extensively. We have to depend heavily on their multiple applications — for purposes of governance, implanting varieties of instructional design, creation of course materials, programme delivery and learner management (registration through certification), i.e. to incorporate e-governance, e-management as well as e-support for learners to take care of all the operations involved in the process. At least one SOU, namely BAOU, Ahmedabad (*see* Sub-section 1.9), has made courageous strides in the process of adopting ICTs for its varied services — other OUs must follow the example. Facilitating cooperation and collaboration in the process of utilising and managing ICTs could be one of the major responsibilities of the proposed National Forum of the OUs in India (*see* Recommendation 1).
6. *Vibrancy of the Faculty and other Staff:* The distinction made between the teachers and other academics within the OU staff structure (*see* Sub-section 1.12) has created more problems than it has solved — worst of all it has infused indifference in certain sections of the staff fraternity. It is time that the related nomenclature and the corresponding responsibilities as well as the related perks are revisited and a reasonably workable structure is agreed to and implemented. Besides, we should not lose sight of so stark a fact that each person who joins an OU as staff, whatever the category, is a novice, and should be treated as such. To make such personnel productively functional, all the OUs should provide opportunities for the older staff to upgrade their skills and know-how, as the system they are working in has to be dynamic. The staff development activities, covering all the levels of staff everywhere within the operational structure of an OU, should be trained as part of policy. It needs to be recognised that it is crucial for the

success and growth of the system. It must be emphasised here that most of the existing and emerging weaknesses of the ODL system in the country cannot be attributed to the system itself; they often originate with, spread from and take roots through those who run the system. Creating a culture of quality in the system is the function of those who manage it — grooming them for the purpose and monitoring their inputs to ensure accountability, have to be ensured, not only to develop the system, but also to sustain that development.

7. *Regulator and Authority for Accreditation*: Creation of an independent regulator to implement the National Policies pertaining to the OUs and ODL operations is already on the cards. The process should be expedited to eliminate the prevailing ad hoc arrangements as soon as possible. This is a significant task, though outside the domain of the OUs, it impinges them most. The MHRD needs to intervene immediately to stop them aligning of the ODL. With unquestionable authority to work with, the tasks which the new regulating body needs to undertake expediently are: i) overhaul the existing regulations, remove all the cobwebs therein and streamline them in purposeful consultation with the National Forum of the OUs, ii) address the confusion and disarray caused by the judgements issued by various courts, iii) streamline the staffing structures for the OUs, iv) ensure appropriate funding patterns, while streamlining the existing ones, to have the burden shared proportionately by the Centre and the respective States, and v) make sure that the spirit as well as the purport of the seminal documents pertaining to ODL system are brought to fruition. These tasks can be addressed effectively with long lasting impact only and only if the related solutions are grounded in a clearly outlined context. This could be provided by means of a well thought out and clearly stated *National Policy on Open Distance Education*, or should we say *National Policy on Flexible Education.* The said policy, for obvious reasons, should precede any action on the tasks listed above.

   Here we need to make a special mention of the Issues related to the recognition of the OU credentials and the accreditation of their courses/ programmes. Given the confusion and the state of, uncertainty created by recent pronouncements of various regulating authorities and courts, it is advisable that the issues pertaining to: i) the recognition of the credentials awarded by the OUs and other ODL institutions which are not constituents of any conventional university, and ii) the accreditation of the courses/ programmes conceived, prepared and launched by the OUs and other ODL institutions should remain a major responsibility of the proposed regulating body. It should also be responsible for the promotion, coordination and maintenance of standards in the ODL system. This responsibility should entail the authority: i) to provide recognition to the credentials awarded by the OUs as well as other ODL institutions, and ii) to work out and legalise multi-level equivalence of the OU credentials with those of the conventional universities and those obtained on the basis of prior learning. Further, it should function as the regulating authority for the ODL operations organised in India by the foreign ODL institutions as well.

22

Reforming the ODL System in India: Recommendations

Commonwealth Educational Media Centre for Asia of Commonwealth of Learning prepared a Report on the Status of State Open Universities in India in 2015. The Report provided an overview of the growth of open education in India. It critically examined the recognition of qualifications, standards and regulations and the preparedness of Open Universities in India for the 21st Century. The Report made recommendations for reforming the ODL system in India. The important parts of recommendations are given below.

Introduction

To serve the needs of Indian society and growing economy, restructuring of the Open Universities (OUs) on a sound basis is the need of the hour. Most of the OUs have been cast in the mould created more than thirty years ago. They are functioning at a primitive level following the norms of the second and third generations of distance education. They are still catering to an old bygone era — an era when what the country required was a workforce suitable for a production-based economy. Today's knowledge-based economy requires the development and preparation of a differently, but highly, skilled and knowledgeable workforce. Our OUs have to cater to this need of the hour and they have the potential to meet the challenge — they need restructuring with this objective at the forefront.

New Agenda for Open Universities

India will remain a young nation and also the largest contributor to the global workforce over the next few decades against the rapidly ageing population in the Western countries as well as China. India is expected to enjoy this benefit until 2040. Accordingly, the Government of India, in line with its forecast of a significant requirement of skilled manpower over the next decade, has set the target of imparting the necessary skills to 500 million people by 2022.

This objective, however, cannot be achieved unless the OUs play their role effectively in imparting training and skills to this target group. The OUs, therefore, need to rededicate and energise themselves to achieve this objective.

India's Economic Goals and ODL

In the coming years, India needs to become one of the largest, if not the largest, talent pool in the world. To achieve this objective, skill and competency-based education needs to be provided. The OUs seem to be the only available mechanism that, used effectively and efficiently, can deliver the goals. For the "Make in India" campaign to succeed, there is a need to make our workforce more competent and more skilled. The OUs can give a definitive fillip to this campaign by providing skill-oriented and competency-based courses along with a mechanism for recognising prior learning and certifying it as well.

Mainstreaming the Ignored Groups

The rural-urban literacy gap which was 21.2 percentage points in 2001 came down to 16.1 percentage points by 2011. But even a gap of 16 percentage points is alarming and needs to be bridged. The OUs, therefore, need to extend their outreach to the rural populations and bring them into the mainstream.

Significantly, the bulk of the labour force in India, about 93 per cent, works in the unorganised sector largely untouched by any kind of formal training. The OUs should make concerted efforts to tap the vast majority of the labour force and upgrade their skills to help improve their productivity. In the process they will also prepare more people with higher skills needed in the organised/ formal sector.

The remodelled OUs should, aim at the development of human and knowledge resources as envisioned by the Planning Commission in its "India Vision of 2020" document. In this document, the Planning Commission has envisaged that "by 2020, the people of India will be more numerous, better educated, healthier and more prosperous than at any time in our long history". True it is, today we find healthier and more prosperous people around and larger numbers of educated people who have completed their schooling and are ready for higher education. We are, however, faced with a disparity — while on the one hand the population has increased exponentially, on the other, the growth in the number of conventional higher education institutions has remained inadequate. This has left a large proportion of young population outside the reach of higher education. The ODL system, therefore, needs to extend its access and reach far and wide for target groups left ignored and unattended.

Certification of Prior Learning and Allied Credit Transfer

The OUs are mandated to cater to the needs of diversified learners who are looking not only for the certification of their learning, but also for their integration with the mainstream of higher education. To achieve this dual objective, the modular approach, that the OUs are already following, needs to be coupled with a lateral entry approach supported by a mechanism for smooth prior learning assessment and recognition (PLAR), which will facilitate the entry of those who have no formal education and training, but have acquired usable and productive skills without obtaining the related certification. Such a mechanism will also benefit those who have discontinued their formal education midway for one or the other reason. The OUs should develop an evaluation framework to assess and recognise competencies gained outside the formal system, assign credit values to such competencies, accommodate (on demand) credits gained at other institutions, and aggregate them appropriately to award relevant degrees, diplomas or certificates. This can very well be achieved through of ICTs-based delivery of education together with the acceptance of certification and qualifications obtained using MOOCs and OER.

There is a need to encourage the development of flexible modular programmes, and uniform and standardised core curricula with elements of flexibility to take care of local and regional contexts across all OUs, so as to make credit transfer easy and operational. A major thrust should be to institute a common credit allocation system for programmes and courses offered through both the distance and the conventional modes. This would smooth out the difficulties being faced by distance learners desirous of migrating from an OU to a conventional university to pursue further studies and vice versa.

Adoption of New Pedagogies

The OUs have to cater to three types of learners — digital natives, digital immigrants and digital illiterates. The challenge before them is to deal purposefully with the three groups of learners, whose levels of digital literacy vary significantly. Today learners, rather than simply receiving and memorising information from texts, are demanding education and training through more engaging means, read new technology.

The OUs need to rethink and remodel their operations to provide an enriched learning experience for the present generation of learners. For this, they need to create a learner-friendly environment and adopt the appropriate technology to support it. To ensure their success, besides using the traditional technologies (print, audio and video CDs, television, radio and face-to-face counselling) the OUs should make extensive use of the Internet technology. Each OU should have its own dynamic website with a dedicated LMS and LCMS for each programme offered by it. Further, each OU should have its own e-platform to host all its learning resources on the web and provide online services for its tech-savvy learners.

Adoption of Economically Relevant Curricula

The OUs need to envision new approaches to providing instruction. They should provide for "learning on demand" and "learner-centred instruction" by adopting appropriate technologies for transacting the curriculum and also for supporting the learning endeavour of the learners.

There is a need for the curricula to be progressive and application and skills-oriented so that the knowledge and skills gained can actually be applied in the world of work. There is also an enormous gap between the demand and supply that only the OUs can bridge, if permitted to offer degree programmes in professional, technical and skills-oriented areas. The OUs need to revisit all their programmes and modify the curricula in tune with the requirements of the industry and the job market in general.

The OUs should set a new trend that would help in churning out knowledge workers. Instead of emulating the conventional degree awarding universities, they should focus on designing market-oriented and industry-integrated programmes. Employability of the graduates has to be considered as a key factor in curriculum design. Further, curricula can be strengthened by enriching them with purposeful components such as content for a set of skills in the areas of communication, problem solving, IT, technical and vocational, entrepreneurial capabilities required for employment. Again, the curricula of the new generation programmes should be designed and developed in collaboration with the concerned industry, so that the programmes are not purely theory-based, but practice and application-oriented and above all, need-based (in terms of the employability of the graduates), with clear cut avenues for the appropriate placement of the graduate in a related industry. These programmes should serve as models of 'work integrated learning' leading to awards that clearly state the skills and competencies acquired. The OUs should adopt the policy of providing stipends to the new apprentices to encourage the learners and facilitate the sharpening of the skills acquired.

Twenty-Four Seven Support Services

Learner support services need to be revamped in order to provide them at a scale and a level, which not only promise, but also offer high quality customer services with the objective of complete customer satisfaction and significantly high pass-out rates. The use of technological solutions should be encouraged in all the support services. Such solutions should be driven by the needs of learners together with the range of access they provide and promote. The network of support services should be accessible to all types of learners enrolled in the system. There should be mechanisms for efficient student tracking and improving the retention rates. Apart from the services provided through the network of various Learner Support Centres, namely Regional Centres and Study Centres, all OUs need to move on to technology-based options, so as to provide instant, accurate and timely service to their learners. Further, technology-based solutions should also promote two-way communication. In other words, they should promote learner-teacher interaction which is essential for maintaining motivation, providing feedback, and for diagnosing difficulties and finding solutions for them. Whatever the self-directed learners may do by themselves, whatever the level of their self-motivation and the nature of their interaction with the content provided in the form of SLMs, they remain vulnerable at the point of application. Moreover, interaction among learners themselves is equally important and is recognised as an extremely valuable resource for learning. In fact, skills of successful teamwork are regarded so essential for functioning in today's work environment. Peer group interaction, whether synchronous or asynchronous, encourages the development of expertise and competencies, and also enhances stimulation and motivation. An active platform for peer interaction is a much required facility, which the usual ODL operations have not been able to activate. ICTs can help the OUs in providing this facility for most of their programmes and learners.

ICTs in Programme Design and Delivery

The next logical step would be to convert all the courseware or the major portions of the courseware into e-content. All the existing learning resources, irrespective of the medium they are in, should be converted into e-content, preferably in the form of e-learning modules, which should be Sharable Content Object Reference Model (SCORM) compliant so that they can be reused, revised, remixed, and re-distributed. Further, it is necessary for the OUs to adopt the Creative Commons License and open, standardised end-user-learner oriented architecture through LMS and interactive Web.2 tools. This would ensure pliancy of the learning resources being used and reused as per the design of programme delivery. Also updating and revisions can be effected easily at frequent intervals as per the requirement. Further, this will make it possible for the OUs to allow choices to their learners, who opt to study for a programme fully online, partly online and partly offline, or just offline.

The e-learning modules should not be passive but interactive in design. Each module should be a judicious media mix of text, audio, video and animation. The e-content should be designed in a manner that would allow integration of content with relevant learning activities, so as to enable learners to master the content and develop critical thinking, creativity and decision-making skills. Learners should be engaged in authentic learning through real-life simulations, examples and experiences. The said activities should deepen learners' involvement in the process of learning by engaging them in sound pedagogic activities — answering questions, interpreting different cases or situations, or solving relevant problems. This will make the e-content engaging, motivating and enlightening and, as a result, it will promote active learning. Evaluation of learner achievements could be managed through formal or informal tests, or through self-assessment strategies.

Talking of evaluation, the methods of evaluation, in use today, are often outdated and are designed to test learners' memory regarding the concepts taught, or supposed to have been learnt, instead of testing their ability to apply the learnt concepts in problem solving activities. Consequently, most of the concepts learnt during the academic year are forgotten once examinations are over. Evaluation should help the learners to reflect on what they have been doing and derive useful insights as well as skills in relation to the topic or content. In e-learning the modules should demonstrate a balance among the three components of effective instruction, namely content, practice and feedback.

Creation of an e-Gateway

The purpose of creating an e-Gateway is in tune with the MHRD's National Mission for Education through ICT. There is a vast body of literature on Open and Distance Education in India, scattered in the form of books, articles published in journals, conference proceedings, newspapers and magazines, mimeos, reports, manuals, etc. The idea behind the e-Gateway is to consolidate all that knowledge, filter it and arrange it systematically, so that it may be used and reused by policy makers, administrators, researchers, teachers and anyone anywhere interested in knowing about the ODL system as it operates in India. Further, the distributed repositories available at all the OUs should be linked to this e-Gateway, so that all knowledge resources as well as the whole range of intellectual resources, created by the OUs, are available to the world. It should be managed by a Central Government Agency, i.e. an independent autonomous body which can serve as a national backbone that provides advanced networking capabilities through high bandwidth connectivity. Further, it should be linked with OER worldwide, which can bring the complete range of intellectual resources available in the world to the Indian population and vice versa. Keeping in view the challenges that the ODL system is facing today, the creation of an e-Gateway will help in making a qualitative change in education, an important social institution. Teachers as well as learners will get wider exposure to develop a world perspective so essential in this age of globalisation and internationalisation of higher education.

Introduction of OER and MOOCs

In keeping with the times, the OUs must develop a policy to systematically place e-content as Open Educational Resources (OER). To achieve this objective, they need to develop standards to ensure interoperability, accessibility and reusability of the OER through the adoption of Creative Commons Licence and open, standardised end-user-learner oriented architecture through the adoption of LMS and interactive Web 2.0 tools, as pointed to earlier.

Open sharing and reusing of resources will speed up the development of new learning resources required to serve the needs of the ever growing diverse groups of learners. This will also reduce and prevent duplication of efforts and indirectly save unnecessary expenditure and effort in reinventing the same or similar type of content that is already available. Further, reuse of learning resources developed using public funds is definitely a better return on investments of tax payers' money. Being in the public domain, OER will promote quality consciousness among the content developers and also bring about qualitative changes in educational offerings at all levels and of all types.

The OUs also need to introduce Massive Open Online Courses (MOOCs). Their policy on MOOCs should be contextualised keeping in mind local needs and requirements. In developing MOOCs, priority needs to be given to extensive use of the local or vernacular languages; their relevance to the cultural milieu needs to be ensured; the quality of knowledge and the accuracy of information contained therein should be unquestionable; and, above all, free and easy access to them needs to be ensured at all costs. Selection of courses to be offered as MOOCs should be done with definite objectives in view, very much on the lines of the Incredible India Campaign, by asking institutions to identify courses that would attract both national and overseas clientele. Secondly, local institutions, state-wise, could be asked to identify such courses as would serve the needs of the rural populations living in the hinterland, or any specific target groups as per their needs and requirements. This would suit the socio-economic needs of each state and its diverse population. Further, the said policy should also display a global perspective by highlighting the need to focus on such areas that have a global market as well.

Technology Driven Governance

It should be mandatory for all OUs to go for ICT applications in all their operations. They should each create a separate fully fledged Department of e-Learning with a Director, who should be competent enough to initiate and coordinate the adoption of diverse technological (ICTs based) solutions for the OUs' operations. It will enhance their effectiveness in reaching and serving the diverse and dispersed learner populations, improve the quality of interaction and learner participation in the educational transactions. This will bring about operational transformation in the processes of student registration, support services and learner evaluation.

Vibrancy of Faculty and Staff

There is a strong need for a vibrant faculty and staff at all the SOUs. In addition, there should be well defined paths for promotion and career advancement for the teachers, other academics (including the technical staff) and administrative staff working at the SOUs in line with those available in the higher education system of the country. The SOUs also have other academics, who function as academic administrators and technical staff involved in electronic media production and ICT operations. This is a category of personnel which is non-existent in the conventional universities. Their equivalence with the faculty (i.e. the teachers) and the administrative staff should be clearly spelt out so that: i) they are not deprived of any benefit, and ii) they do not drag along their jobs indifferently.

It should be mandatory for the faculty and the rest of the staff to periodically undergo training for upgrading their skills and know-how, and acquainting them with the latest technological possibilities as well as familiarising them with e-Learning options, not only for purposes of promotions, but also to improve the functioning of the OUs and their services to the learners. Faculty members should be entitled to attend an international conference, a seminar or a workshop once in two years, and a national level conference, seminar or workshop once in a year. Similarly, their visits to regulatory bodies and/ or other ODL institutions at regular intervals should be ensured to promote cross-pollination of ideas and purposeful practices and the consequent growth. The administrative staff, too, should be entitled to attend national conferences, seminars and/ or workshops pertaining to e-Governance, Management, Right to Information (RTI) related themes and the like.

Further, the faculty should be encouraged to undertake research activities for which the SOUs should allocate funds annually for teachers as well as for other academics. To make this thrust meaningful, mechanisms should be in place for research-based outcomes to be ploughed back into the system on a regular basis.

Accreditation of OUs and their Programmes

The time has come to adopt a transnational approach to quality assurance and accreditation and international benchmarking of standards and practices in the emerging borderless world.

The erstwhile DEC did this work and currently the DEB, through its policy regarding the recognition of ODL institutions and their programmes is, in a way, enhancing the quality of the system. The evaluation of quality, as effected under this policy, is more like an external review, which is not enough to ensure quality in all respects. The immediate need to internalise the process of qualitative evaluation is to insist on self-evaluation practices that would account for internal self-audit alongside the external assessment of quality. The creation of a Centre for Internal Quality Assurance (CIQA) at each of the OUs during the Eleventh Plan period (2007-12) was the first step taken in this direction. It was mandated to facilitate the OUs to raise awareness about quality assurance in general and initiate internal review practices that would gradually become embedded in the routine and regular conduct of work. The next logical step is to introduce systematic accreditation of all the ODL providers. It is time to revisit the said first step, ensure that the related operations are in place, and move on to the suggested second step, alongside.

There is an urgent need for a National Accreditation Board specifically for the ODL system in India, as the DEB under the UGC is only an interim arrangement awaiting the creation of an apex body for the purpose by an Act of Parliament. Since the UGC does not have the mandate to accredit institutions other than the universities, all ODL stand alone institutions (that are not universities) are outside the ambit of the DEB, and have no authorised agency to ask for recognition either of their institutions, or their programmes. All conventional universities apply to NAAC for accreditation, but the OUs have never applied to NAAC, as NAAC has not developed any parameters to accredit the ODL institutions.

Ideally, the MHRD should notify all the accredited programmes and display the related comprehensive list on its website. This will provide the much needed transparency, so crucial for all stakeholders and particularly for students and for employers. In the process, no distinction should be made between the conventional and the ODL institutions. As a consequence, the awards obtained through the distance/ ODL mode will not be discriminated against.

Need for a National Policy and an Independent Regulator

The Central Government needs to come up with a National Policy on Open and Distance Learning, which visualises a robust national system of ODL in India. This document should address the concerns of all the sectors and all the levels of education, including basic education, vocational and skills development, continuing professional development in all sectors of the economy, and research and development among other areas. It should outline the operations of the ODL system and its various subsystems as per defined norms and standards. It should look at not only the new technology-supported options available, but also pay attention to the new learning environments in the context of ongoing demographic and cultural changes, and outline proper strategies for better utilisation of the ODL system over the next twenty years. Further, it should provide for the creation of an autonomous regulator 2, responsible for the promotion, coordination and maintenance of standards in the ODL system. Like the University Grants Commission, the proposed autonomous regulator should function directly under the MHRD so as to effectively co-ordinate the efforts of the OUs, the Directorates of Distance Education attached to the conventional universities and the stand alone ODL institutions (that are not universities). The regulator should also concretise the required benchmarks for infusing quality in the system. This mechanism will help in introducing and sustaining the culture of self-accountability, ensuring mandatory accreditation of all ODL providers based on international benchmarks, bringing credibility to the ODL system in India, and also in investing it with the recognition it deserves. The system will then stand out as an accepted mode, alongside the conventional formal system, capable of providing not only extensive access, but also of fulfilling the mandate of expansion, inclusion and excellence.

The said National Policy should insist on the autonomous regulator instilling a culture of quality in the ODL system, from its top to bottom, by initiating the following steps:

- Discipline-wise norms and standards for offering programmes through the distance mode need to be developed by the autonomous regulator in collaboration with the existing statutory bodies working in various sectors of the country. These norms should cover all levels and types of programmes ranging from awareness and certificate level to doctoral degree programmes. All major disciplines including professional and technical must be covered, while priority should be given to the latter as there is a great demand for professional and technical education.
- Research and development are crucial activities in an era that is essentially driven by knowledge and information. The

advancement of systemic research is essential for bringing about improvements in and credibility to the system. The autonomous regulator should prepare guidelines on how to provide an environment conducive for such research and development. Innovations and innovative ideas need to be institutionally facilitated with structures like incubation centres, research chairs, recognition and awards for the faculty who make tangible contributions to research and development.

- The autonomous regulator should be given the mandate to sanction posts and fund them too. Further, staff development activities (encouraging innovation in curriculum design, instructional design, programme delivery, learner support and evaluation), involving academics and non-academics alike, should be yet another area of concern for the autonomous regulator. For this purpose, clear cut policies need to be established for the faculty and other staff of the OUs with a view to promoting and fostering a student-centred system.
- The autonomous regulator should promote and ensure transparency in admissions, development and delivery of academic programmes, student evaluation and declaration of results. Broad guidelines have to be drawn up for good governance of different types of ODL institutions.
- The time has come to adopt a transnational approach to quality assurance and accreditation and international benchmarking of standards and practices in the emerging borderless world. This is an imperative now, as we need to bring under the umbrella of our national regulations even those foreign ODL providers who are operating in India. The autonomous regulator should frame guidelines and policies to cover them and monitor their work and contributions.

All the initiatives outlined above, and proposed to be undertaken by the autonomous regulator, will require tremendous collaborative efforts in terms of critical thinking, software development, human resources and funding, which the Ministry of Human Resource Development would need to organise and provide in order to restructure and strengthen the ODL system in the country.

Ultimately the role of the autonomous regulator should become that of a "facilitator" rather than that of a typical "regulator". It should be able to stimulate both public and private providers to establish their own self-regulatory mechanisms to weed out bad and indifferent practices and promote excellence and quality in the system.

23

National Conference Recommendations

Symbiosis Centre for Distance Learning, Pune, organised National Conference on Distance and Online Learning in 2014. The Conference was attended by around 100 distinguished delegates across the country comprising policy makers, including registrars, directors of distance education institutions, senior professors, etc. The conference had the following themes:

- Government Policies for ODL – Future Path
- Role of ODL in Building GER
- Paradigm from Conventional Education to Online Learning
- Issues and Challenges with Present System: Path towards Online Learning
- Emerging Trends in ODL
- International Best Practices

Each plenary session was followed by a Question-Answer session and the conference ended with discussion on policy recommendations.

The recommendations are given here for the benefit of readers.

Territorial Jurisdiction

- Open and distance education is the need of the hour to increase the GER in a young country such as India, since it provides equity and access to education at a cost which is about one-fifth the cost incurred in the conventional education system.
- It is the only answer to reach the unreached and physically, economically, socially and locationally disadvantaged people.
- Technology has been a "game changer" bringing about a paradigm shift in the teaching-learning process, in the mode of delivery of the teaching pedagogy and evaluation methodologies.
- In a scenario of smart phones, tablets, access to international educational qualifications, availability of online programs and courses (e.g. MOOC), and territorial jurisdiction for distance learning institutions has lost its relevance.
- Since technology has made 'anyone, anywhere, anytime education' possible "geography" has become "history" in the world of open and distance learning; therefore raising the issue

of territorial jurisdiction for distance learning institutions would defeat the very purpose that these institutions are expected to fulfill in achieving the objective of the government and the notion of increasing the GER, reaching the unreached, and providing higher education to the masses at their doorstep in a cost-effective manner.

- Thus, if all the components namely, Admission Learning Management System (LMS), counselling, submission of assignments and, evaluation and final examination of the ODL programme are offered completely online, then the question of restriction on territorial limits would be irrelevant.
- It is, therefore, recommended that the UGC relooks at its policy on territorial jurisdiction taking into consideration on the various points highlighted above.

Quality

- Increased confidence in the integrity of Online Distance Learning (ODL) needs to be built with the recognition and accreditation of distance learning programmes by an independent academic accreditation body.
- There is a need to define the qualifications and skill sets for faculty engaged in distance-learning activity towards an outcome-based assessment.
- Proper measures should be taken for training and capacity building of its faculty and administrative staff at regular intervals.
- ODL institutions need to keep pace with the latest developments in information technology and widening skill gaps.
- ODL institutions to provide flexibility in teaching-learning and evaluation processes that fit work schedules of lifelong learners.
- There is a need for two-way synchronous learning using audio and video conferencing an online replica of a classroom.
- State-of-the-art infrastructure learning management system, digital library, student-support service, broadband connectivity, etc. needs to be made available.
- There is a need to have internal quality assurance structures in place in every ODL institution.
- Good quality of e-books and a digital library should be given due emphasis by ODL institutions.
- Academic programmes, should be designed in such a manner that they provide learners with a sufficient range of transferable skills to enable them to play a more important role when they

enter employment. The nomenclature of the degrees/ diplomas proposed to be awarded through such programmes should be approved by the regulatory authorities. Easily accessible high-quality self-learning material and the ICT backbone could enhance access and e-governance in the ODL system and enable interactive learning and dissemination of knowledge through all modes (print, audio-visual and Internet-based multimedia). The regulatory authority could collaborate with the National Mission on Education through ICT to avail of the web-based high-quality educational resources being developed by it. It should also endeavour to develop a sharable pool of self-learning material.

- ODLs could get their SLMs examined and certified by external experts before a programme is launched to ensure quality.
- Quality in evaluation system should be maintained through developing good-quality assessment tools; there could be a pooling of resources by the ODL institutions in order to achieve the same.
- Every ODL institution should have a built-in system of obtaining feedback from the students on all aspects of its operations, from the design of the programme, its delivery mechanisms, and teaching-learning to the evaluation process, and ensure that it uses the inputs so obtained to improve its quality by bridging gaps, if any.
- Every ODL institution should establish an Internal Quality Assurance Cell (IQAC) to ensure the quality of its programmes through an internal self-regulatory and monitoring mechanism.
- Training programmes for faculty for developing questions for the computerised testing system can be organised by the regulator.
- ODL institution should integrate online with traditional face-to-face classroom activities in a planned and pedagogical manner in both synchronous and asynchronous modes, which may include virtual classes, online faculty interaction sessions, facilities to learn through e-learning, recorded sessions, prerecorded lectures and personal contact programmes, OERs, etc.
- Finally, there is a need for a change in the mindset of all stakeholders, particularly, regulators and service providers as well as service recipients quality on a continuing basis comes only through its demand from the service recipients

Evaluation

- Assessment should be both formative as well as summative. Formative assessment should be through tutor-marked assignment projects, seminars, hands-on experience, and practicals linked to the objectives and desired competencies/ skills, or expected learning outcomes.
- Tools of assessment should be prepared by empanelled expats and widely publicised.
- All tools of assessment should be moderated before being administered to ensure reliability and validity and standards as per the level of the programme.
- Preparation of ideal responses for assignments as well as summative assessments should be supplied to evaluators.
- Examinations should be held at my centre identified by the ODL institution.
- Use of a common exam form for all courses and programmes should be instituted.
- Accurate compilation/ tabulation of grades/ marks by the exam unit for each learner, course-wise needs be maintained.
- Measures should be taken for fair conduct of examinations, such as deputing of observers, sending of flying squads, etc.
- Times schedules should be adhered to, particularly in the declaration of results.
- Accuracy/ authentication of certification should be ensured.
- An item bank repository, with a variety of attributes namely, difficulty level, type, marks, associated learning units, etc., should be maintained by ODL institutions.
- ODL should explore the possibility of conducting examination using ICT.
- ODL institutions wishing to conduct Ph.D programmes should ensure that they have an adequate number of eligible guides as per the norms of the regulator. These should be guides who are permanent members of the faculty of such an institution in that particular broad area of study.
- Prior sanction of the regulator could be obtained by giving the necessary details with regard to the faculty, digital library, etc., and could get their ordinances related to programmes in place.
- An ODL instituted desirous of introducing a Ph.D programme could have a Research and Recognition Committee with eminent experts in the field of research to examine and approve research proposals.

Faculty

- The qualifications and skill set required by a faculty teaching in a distance learning institute should be clearly defined.
- The number of faculty required in an ODL institution should be based on norms, which take into account the requirements of all ODL institutions, rather than the faculty norms of a conventional university.
- There could be training and orientation programmes conducted by the Government to train the faculty in the skill sets required by an ODL institution.
- There could be more programmes in teacher education to train teachers to teach through the distance mode aimed at qualifying them to teach in an ODL institution.

Regulatory Mechanism

- There is a widespread feeling both among higher education authorities and distance education providers that the system is in urgent need of management and regulatory reform, if it has to fulfill the increasing demand of learners for access and quality.
- A system of self-disclosure of the details which are spelt out by the regulator should be followed by an ODL institution. It could include information about its programme details course delivery, particulars of its faculty and support staff, and information pertaining to learner centres, its enrollments, registrations, re-registrations, working hours feedback mechanisms, and exam related data, other than learning outcomes of students, new progranmes launched, details of collaborative arrangements with other institutions, and details of degrees awarded.
- Proper quality standards can be laid down by the regulator.
- As the syllabi and the exanimations are common for conventional as well as ODL systems in dual-mode institutions, the degree imparted through the ODL system should be treated at par with the conventional system, both for education as well as employment purpose. However for the purpose of record, the degree/ certificate of the ODL learner should mention 'Through Distance Mode' or 'Through Online' as the case may be, on its face.

Delivery Mechanism

- The SLM should have clearly stated objectives, intended learning outcomes, study guidance and advice for learners on how to optimally use the SLM and suggested reference material to enhance his/ her learning experience Linkages within the text with other media should be maintained for easy referencing and progress.

- The SLM should provide an adequate mechanism for learners to provide feedback on their understanding of the subject.
- The SLM should be revised at such intervals of time as may be prescribed by the regulator.
- The SLM should be in multiple media such as in the print form, audio and video programmes, digital media, and online-interactive modules.
- ODL institutions should be permitted to provide soft copies of SLMs to distance learners, and printed SLMs could be made available for those students who are not tech-savvy or are digitally disadvantaged. Making available soft copies would be a soc-friendly measure to save paper, as well as costs to distant learners, while at the same time, enabling ODL institutions to make frequent upgrades of their programmes and content without worrying about costs.
- An ODL should manage teaching-learning activities through online support for interactive learning with learner feedback, to facilitate the use of Open Educational Resources (OER), Massive Open Online Courses (MOOC), and for continuous as well as term-end evaluation, certification, and other student support.
- In an ODL system, technology is game changer bringing about a paradigm shift in the manner in which the teaching-learning process is being conducted in a scenario of 'anywhere, anytime education', where the student has the flexibility for credit banking and for multiple point entry and exit, and an opportunity is provided to a student to learn at his own pace, virtual classes and video conferencing or online faculty interactions, e-learning material, pre-recorded lectures, etc., are replacing face-to-face teaching. Similarly, use of technology to conduct examinations through online exams reduces the need for the subjective element in the examination.

Student Support

- Induction programmes, at the beginning of each academic year, need to be conducted.
- Academic support can be provided through virtual classroom sessions, academic counselling, vocational guidance, hands-on experience, library services, e-Learning material, prerecorded lecture DVDs, e-books, PCPs, printed SLMs, etc.

- Organisation of counselling sessions should be done course-wise. Learners should be made aware of the support services provided to them through programme guides, brochures letters, website, emails, SMS on mobiles, online chats, virtual mode on telephone, etc.
- Examination and evaluation-related queries should be addressed immediately and norms for the timeframe within which the results need to be declared need to be spelt out.
- Non-academic queries of a student pertaining to various processes of the ODL institute with Regard to the payment of fees, booking for exam, or booking for a virtual session, etc. need to be addressed and communicated to the student.
- Organised learner support need to be provide through study centres established and maintained by the university/ institution at existing recognised educational institutions. These study centres should be equipped to provide both academic and administrative support services, such as dissemination of information, academic counselling (for both theory and practical courses), vocational guidance, hands-on experience, multimedia support, library services, evaluation of assignments, feedback, guidance of project work, organisation of seminars field trips, conduct of term-end exams, monitoring, etc.
- Pre-admission counselling for prospective learners should be done to provide information to facilitate them in taking an informed decision on joining a specific ODL programme
- Support should be provided for admission-related matters.
- Arrangements should be made to ensure the delivery of study material to learners within a fortnight from the dates of admission.
- There should be a full-time and dedicated help desk well versed with learner-information database providing single-window service for all learner-related quries.

24

University Grants Commission (Open and Distance Learning) Regulations, 2017

University Grants Commission issued new regulations on 23 March 2017. The regulations are in five parts and in eleven Annexures as indicated below:

Part-1: Recognition of Higher Education Institutions for Open and Distance Learning Programmes.

Part-2: Maintenance of Infrastructural Academic and other Quality Standards by Higher Educational Institutions.

Part-3: Admissions, Examinations and Learner Support

Part-4: Assessment, Accreditation, Audit, Inspection and Monitoring.

Part-5: Miscellaneous

Annexure – I : Centre for Internal Quality Assurance.

Annexure – II : Quality Monitoring Mechanism

Annexure – III : Minimum Standards to be maintained at Examination Centres.

Annexure – IV : Courses or Study Centres or off Campus and Territorial Jurisdiction of Universities.

Annexure – V : Competencies of Counsellors in a Learning Support Centre.

Annexure – VI : Academic and Infrastructural Requirements.

Annexure - VII : Quality Assurance Guidelines of Learning Material, Human Resource, Curriculum and Pedagogy.

Annexure –VIII : Guidelines on Preparation of Self-Learning Material.

Annexure – IX : Guidelines on Programme Project Report.

Annexure – X : Learner Support Centre.

Annexure – XI : Grievance Redressal Mechanism.

Some significant guidelines are detailed below

Centre for Internal Quality Assurance (CIQA)

The objective of establishment of Centre for Internal Quality Assurance (CIQA) is to develop and put in place a comprehensive and dynamic internal quality assurance system to provide high quality programmes of higher education in the Open and Distance Learning mode. Its functions would inter alia include the following:

i. To maintain quality in the services provided to the learners.
ii. To ensure continuous improvement in the entire operations of the Higher Educational Institution.
iii. To identify the key areas in which the Higher Educational Institution should maintain quality.
iv. To disseminate information on quality assurance.
v. To devise mechanisms for interaction and obtaining feedback from various Departments or Centres or Schools in the Higher Educational Institution.
vi. To suggest to the authorities of the Higher Educational Institution, measures for qualitative improvement.
vii. To ensure the implementation of its recommendations through regular monitoring.
viii. To ensure participation of all stakeholders namely, learners, teachers, staff, parents, society, employers, and Government in quality improvement processes.
ix. To prepare Programme Project Report and ensure another launch of programme(s).
x. Collection, collation and dissemination of accurate, complete and reliable statistics about the quality of the programme(s).

To fulfill the above objectives the Centre for Internal Quality Assurance shall:

i. prepare a Programme Project Respect for each programme according to the norms and guidelines prescribed by the Commission and necessary by the appropriate regulatory authority having control over the programme;
ii. get the Prograrmme Project Report approved by the authority of the Higher Educational Institution and the Commission before launch of the programme;
iii. oversee the development of Study Learning Material (SLM), integration of Information and Communication Technology (ICT), setting up of Learning Centres and coordination with the parent institution and relevant Regulatory authorities;
iv. put in place monitoring mechanism to ensure the proper implementation of Programme Project Reports;
v. design annual plans for quality level enhancement at the level of the Higher Educational Institution and ensure their implementation;
vi. arrange for feedback responses from students, employers and other stakeholders for quality related institutional processes;
vii. develop quality benchmarks or parameters for the various academic and administrative activities of the Higher Educational Institution;

viii. obtain information from other Higher Educational Institutions on various quality benchmarks or parameters and best practices;

ix. organise workshops or seminars on quality related themes and Higher Educational Institution wise dissemination of the proceedings of such activities;

x. suggest restructuring of programmes in order to make them relevant to the job market;

xi. develop and implement innovative practices in major areas leading to quality enhancement in services to the learners;

xii. create learner centric environment rather than institution centric environment;

xiii. cultivate creativity and innovation in the faculty and staff;

xiv. adopt measures to ensure intemalisation and institutionalisation of quality enhancement practices through periodic accreditation and audit;

xv. conduct or encourage system based research to bring about qualitative change in the entire system;

xvi. coordinate between the Higher Educational Institution and the Commission for various quality related issues or guidelines;

xvii. record activities undertaken on quality assurance in the form of an annual report; and

xviii. to coordinate recognition and accreditation of the Higher Educational Institution.

It will be mandatory for all Higher Educational Institution to submit Annual Report to its Statutory Authorities or Bodies about the activities undertaken by Centre for Internal Quality Assurance during the financial year.

Establishment of Centre for Internal Quality Assurance

The Centre for Internal Quality Assurance will be established in all Higher Educational Institutions offering programmes in Open and Distance Learning mode and should be headed by a full-time Director, being a senior academician of the rank of Professor, who shall be supported by adequate number of academic and other staff.

A Centre for Internal Quality Assurance Committee should be constituted which shall be chaired by its Director, and consisting of academic staff and internal quality auditors nominated from various functions or departments of the Higher Educational Institution. It shall perform following functions:

i. decide policies for programme development methodology and programme delivery mechanism that are aligned with the vision and mission of the Higher Educational Institution;

ii. advise on any issues related to programme development, Information and Communication Technology intervention and implementation, learning and teaching, collaboration referred to the Committee;

iii. Supervise academic approval and related modification procedures and to ensure that programmes satisfy stated design requirements and academic standards appropriate to the type and level of award as per philosophy of the Open and Distance Learning mode of education;

iv. promote automation of academic and administrative activities of the Higher Educational Institution, Regional Centres and Study Centres or Learning Support Centres;

v. Oversee and report on the effectiveness of systems for self-evaluation and monitoring;

vi. appoint external subject experts or agencies or organisations for validation and annual review of its in-house process, its Learner Support Centres, Open and Distance Learning mode programmes, etc.;

vii. appoint third party auditing bodies for quality audit of programme(s);

viii. approval of Self-Appraisal Report to be submitted to the Assessment and Accreditation agencies on behalf of Higher Educational Institution;

ix. Promote collaboration and association for quality enhancement of Open and Distance Learning mode of education and research therein; and

x. encourage industrial involvement and industry-institution linkage for providing exposure to the learners.

Quality Monitoring Mechanism

The guidelines on quality monitoring mechanism are required to be adopted by Centre for Internal Quality Assurance for conducting institutional quality audits, to promote quality assurance and enhance as well as spread best-in-class practices of quality assurance. Quality monitoring needs to be addressed under the following broad areas, namely

(a) *Governance, Leadership and Management*

This relates to the policies and practices of Higher Educational Institutions (HEIs) in the matter of planning, human resources, recruitment, training, performance appraisal, financial management and the overall role of leadership, with a focus on the following key aspects:

i. *Organisation Structure and Governance*: The Higher Educational Institution is ultimately responsible for quality programmes and learning outcomes. Therefore, it is required that the Institution should fill all required positions in the Directorate or Centre or Department and in the Learner Support Centres as prescribed by the Commission, and establish a credible governance system.

ii. *Management*: Effective leadership by setting values and participative decision-making process is the key to achieve the vision, mission and goals of the Higher Educational Institution. Therefore, it is required to assess and review the organisational culture to support the management and leadership of the institution to achieve such vision, mission and goals.

iii. *Strategic Planning*: The leadership of the Higher Educational Institution is expected to provide clear vision and mission. Its functions are to be governed by the principles of participation and transparency. Therefore, the Higher Educational Institution is expected to do strategic planning of its activities and implementing by aligning those with academic and administrative aspects to improve the overall quality.

iv. *Operational Plan, Goals and Policies*: The Higher Educational Institutions derives the operational plan from its strategic plan that defines targets and measures of the programmes to be achieved by the Institution. The Operational Plan is used as a guideline for the annual planning of programmes and activities. The Higher Educational Institution needs to have well defined goals which are realistic and measurable. Equally important is to have well-defined policies that are in sync with its strategic plan and are realistic and achievable. The Higher, Educational Institution needs to have clearly stated guidelines in the implementation of its policies and plans. Further, the institution needs to have a transparent and accountable system for its policies and planning that are well communicated to its stakeholders.

(b) *Articulation of Higher Educational Institution's Objectives*

The Higher Educational Institutions are expected to provide holistic and quality education with a professional focus, the creation of knowledge and innovation, and the practical application of the knowledge to support the business and professional community. Accordingly, the Higher Educational Institution should articulate a clear vision, mission, ethos and broad strategy consistent with the goals to strengthen its position for offering programmes in Open and Distance Learning mode.

(c) *Programme Development and Approval Processes*

This area of concern relates to programme development and approval mechanism for the programme(s) to be lunched, covering the following key aspects:

i. *Curriculum Design*: The Higher Educational Institution plays the foremost role in the curriculum design and development of learning content and, therefore, it is expected to have processes, systems and structures in place to carry these responsibilities. Curriculum design is a process of developing appropriate need-based curriculum in consultation with expert groups, based on the feedback from stakeholders, resulting in the development of relevant programmes with flexibility, to suit the professional and personal needs of the learner and realisation of core values. The key aspect is also to consider the good practices of the Institution in initiating a range of programme options and courses that are relevant to the local needs and in tune with the emerging national and global trends.

ii. *Curriculum Planning and Implementation*: It is required that the Higher Educational Institution shall have specific implementation plans for identifying the time to be spent on specific components of the implementation phase. It is the basis for the effectiveness of the programme(s) and their usefulness as a whole.

iii. *Academic Flexibility*: Academic flexibility is the key feature of the Open and Distance Learning mode of education and refers to freedom in the use of the time-frame of courses, vertical mobility, and inter-disciplinary options facilitated by curricular transactions. Therefore, the Higher Educational Institution shall adopt proper strategies for imparting academic flexibility.

iv. *Learning Resource*: Learning Resource is a key component of the Open and Distance Learning mode of education. Learning resource can be of print and digital mode. Considering the need of blended learning, the Higher Educational Institution should also develop e-resources for the learner to refer and study. There is no or very little interaction of teachers with the learners, the content and structure of learning resources play a vital role in the Open and Distance Learning mode of education. Therefore, it is required that each Higher Educational Institution shall ensure the quality of learner resources and their periodical review. While deciding on the appropriateness of the media and the technologies, the Higher Educational Institution should take into consideration various factors – the media and technology utilised matches the course content in order to enhance and expand learning, and to match to the learners' needs; that these are accessible, practical and equitable, and cost effective to the learners.

v. *Feedback System:* The process of revision and redesign of curricula shall be based on recent market dynamics, industrial developments, research and feedback from the stakeholders including learners. The feedback from all stakeholders in terms of its relevance and appropriateness in cantering to the society, economy and environment are also considered in this key aspect.

Programme Monitoring and Review

The Higher Educational Institution shall plan and execute programme monitoring review system which should include a programme management structure, annual programme reviews, external benchmarking, channels for collecting learner feedback, and development of improvement plans and actions to close the feedback. To maintain the quality of academic programme, it is required to conduct periodical internal reviews. For such reviews the Institution shall also consider achievements of learning outcomes that are assessed through the examination system.

(e) *Infrastructure Resources*

This criterion seeks to elicit data on the adequacy and optimal use of the facilities available in a university or institution to maintain the quality of academic and other programmes-physical facilities, library (or e-library), Information Technology infrastructure, etc. It also requires information on how every constituent of the Institution; the learners, teachers or Counsellors and staff benefits from these facilities.

(f) *Learning Environment and Learner Support*

The learner support unit is responsible for the delivery of services to all learners. The learner support services including library services shall be accessed electronically by the learner. "Physical library" and classroom environment is the core requirement for programme delivery through offline and blended mode. Additionally, Higher Educational Institution shall establish virtual facilities as component of the learning environment which are focused around the pedagogical use of modern educational practices to support blended learning. Learner Support Services shall be provided through the campus-wide portal and e-Learning platform. The Institution shall take a more sophisticated approach to the use of Information and Communication Technology and expertise in e-Learning. The approach shall provide a seamless learner-centred environment.

(g) *Assessment and Evaluation*

Learning outcomes are the specifications of what a Learner shall learn and demonstrate on successful completion of the course or the programme. It can also be seen as the desired outcome of the learning process in terms of acquisition of the skills and knowledge. They are embedded in the curriculum. Achieving Learning Outcomes needs specific experiences to be provided to the learners and evaluation of their attainment. The Institution needs to ensure that the purposes of assessment are clearly described in the course materials, and the learners are able to access some of the assignments. A programme that states Learning Outcomes that are not evaluated or assessed gets neglected in implementation. Hence all the stated Learning Outcomes must be part of the evaluation protocol of the programme. Learner assessment provides an indication of the areas where learning has happened and where it has to be improved upon. The Higher Educational Institutions shall execute the assessment and evaluation through varied assessment tools including multiple choice questions, projects, reports, case studies, presentations, and term-end examinations, to suit the different learning outcomes expected of the course elements. The Higher Educational Institutions shall have proper assessment and moderation system for assessing the learning outcomes of learners.

(h) *Teaching Quality and Staff Development*

The Higher Educational Institutions shall have a well established structure for promoting quality counselling and provide staff development programmes and activities to encourage academic staff to improve teaching and learning. The Higher Educational Institution should provide the support for the academic staff in understanding and implementing the institutional learning outcomes and subject learning outcomes. The Institution also needs to ensure that the academic staff is conversant with formative and summative assessment procedures and their importance in the learning process.

Regulating Provisions

(A) *University Grants Commission Regulations on Private Universities*

A private university established under a State Act shall be a unitary University. A private university may be permitted to open off-campus centres, off-shore campuses and study centres after five years of its coming into existence subject to the fulfillment of conditions as laid down under University Grants Commission (Establishment of & Maintenance of Standards in Private Universities) Regulations, 2003. As of now, the University Grants Commission has not granted permission to any private university to establish off-campus or study centre.

(B) *University Grants Commission Regulations on Deemed Universities*

A Deemed University shall operate only within its Headquarters or from those off-campuses or off-shore campuses which are approved by the Government of India through notification published in the Official Gazette.

In case of distance education programmes, no institution deemed to be university, so declared by the Government of India after 26 May 2010 [date of publication of University Grants Commission (Institutions Deemed to be Universities) Regulations, 2010] is allowed to conduct courses in the distance mode.

The institutions deemed to be universities declared before 26 May 2010 are not allowed to conduct courses in distance mode from any of its off campus centres or off-shore campuses approved after 26 May 2010.

Approval for new courses and extension of approval of the courses already run by the Deemed to be Universities under distance mode would be granted by the University Grants Commission subject to the fulfillment of conditions as laid down by the University Grants Commission.

The University Grants Commission has not granted approval to any deemed to be university to establish study centres.

Any information or clarification with regard to recognition of private universities or deemed universities and the courses offered by them may be obtained from JS (CPP-I) University Grants Commission, Bahadurshah Zafar Marg, New Delhi-110002.

(C) *Distance Education programmes of the Central Universities and State Government Universities*

The Central or State Government Universities can conduct courses through distance mode in accordance with the provisions of their respective Act and after the approval of the University Grants Commission.

Competencies of Counsellor in a Learner Support Centre

1. Should be a post graduate from a Recognised University.
2. Familiarity with basic research on the characteristics of Distance Learners, their needs and difference from conventional face-to-face education.
3. Application of basic principles of instructional design.
4. Thorough knowledge of subject matter and common misconceptions related to the course(s).

5. Deep understanding of the necessity of learner-centered environment in online and blended learning mode.
6. Ability to design constructivist learning environment.
7. Practical applications of learning theories, self-paced instruction, and computer-mediated communication and learning.
8. Ability to foster a sense of community among learners.
9. Adaptability and flexibility with the capabilities and limitations of the delivery media.
10. Familiarity with the delivery medium to provide basic troubleshooting.
11. Ability to multitask.
12. Time management (e.g. respond to learners in timely manner, extensive and advance preparation and planning).
13. Professional characteristics (e.g motivated to teach, self-confident, articulate, good writer).

Quality Assurance Guidelines of Learning Material in Multiple Media, Human Resource, Curriculum and Pedagogy

1. Learning Material (Print Media)

Learning Material through print-media is termed as Self Learning Material, being developed with the approach of self-explanatory, self-contained, self-directed, self-motivating and self-evaluating. The following is an indicative list of quality standards for print material:

a) The Self Learning Material shall be designed with the approach of two-way communication between the learner and content.
b) The Self Learning Material shall involve the learner actively through various experience-based activities and assignments.
c) The learner should get clear information about the structure of the programme and course.
d) There shall be detail learning map in Self Learning Material for the learners so that he or she will be self-directed for completion of his or her studies.
e) The content of Self Learning Material shall be developed with dialogue and personal system of writing method which will create the nature of interactivity in Self Learning Material.
f) The Self Learning Material shall encourage learner to apply new knowledge and skills.
g) There shall be clear definition of learning objectives and outcomes.
h) The content shall be divided into small sections (blocks) and sub-sections (units and sub-units) for effective learning.

i) There shall be an assignment on each learning objective for self-assessment.

j) The learner shall be directed through problem solving activities as applicable to nature of the course.

k) The Self Learning Material shall be developed in defined formats with following features:

(i) Consistent layout and format.

(ii) Inclusion of overview of content.

(iii) A unit structure at the beginning of the unit.

(iv) Plenty of examples.

(v) Reference to prior learning.

(vi) Inclusion of national or international caselets and case studies.

(vii) Content in segments synchronised with learning objectives and outcome.

(viii) Explanation of icons used in content.

(ix) Appropriate sequence of material.

(x) Explanation on technical, new, difficult terms or word in a glossary section.

(xi) Inclusion of adequate suggested reading (both print and online).

2. *Audio-video Material: Quality Standards*

a) There shall be adequate consideration of learners' prior knowledge skills and attitudes.

b) Level and style of language shall be appropriate.

c) There shall be clear information on types of support material and study activities to be used by the learner.

d) It shall be clear and unambiguous also preferably free from pedagogic jargon.

e) The aim, objective and target audience for the Audio Video material shall be clearly defined.

f) It shall be capable of being evaluated to conform to the learning outcomes.

g) There shall be clear guidelines with regard to the use of the Audio or Visual material vis-a-vis other content of the course.

h) Audio Video material shall be developed in forms and formats that will be easily accessible by the learners.

i) There shall be separate Audio Video manual for giving the guidelines of using the Audio Video material in study.

j) Audio Video material shall provide continuity and coherence within and between audio-based study sessions.

k) There shall be synchronisation of sound and image in Audio Video material.
l) There shall be appropriate graphics and animations relevant to the course content.
m) There shall be appropriate 'visual texture' and rate of change of image to keep the learner involved.

3. *Online Material: Quality Standards*

a) The course shall be organised into units and lessons.
b) There shall be description of unit overview along with objectives, activities, assignments and resources that frame the unit.
c) Availability of a programme map and correlation matrix among the courses in the programme.
d) There shall be description of credit value of each module or unit in the course.
e) There shall be clear guidelines on academic integrity and netiquette (internet etiquette) expectations regarding lesson activities, discussions and plagiarism.
f) There shall be lesson overview, content and activities, assignments to provide the learning opportunities for learner to master the content.
g) The course shall be designed to teach concepts and skills that the learner will retain throughout the study.
h) There shall be multiple learning paths for engaging the learner in active learning
i) The content shall provide opportunities for learners to engage in high-order thinking, critical-reasoning activities and thinking in increasing by complex ways.
j) There shall be appropriate readability levels, written language assignments and mathematical requirements.
k) The content shall provide for periodical feedback about the learning process.
l) The course shall be easy to navigate.
m) There shall be declaration of textbooks, courseware, and online resources necessary to refer additionally to complete the course.
n) The content shall be accessible on various devices.
o) The online material shall satisfy the needs of learners with disabilities.

4. *Computer-based Material: Quality Standards*

a) The Computer-based material shall provide an environment for practice, at the learner's own pace and in his own time.
b) The Computer-based material shall provide an environment for self-assessment.
c) It shall allow learners to develop analysis and decision-making skills, to discover principles and concepts for themselves.
d) The course shall be organised into units and lessons.
e) There shall be description of unit overview along with objectives, activities, assignments and resources that frame the unit.
f) Availability of a programme map and correlation matrix among the courses in the programme.
g) There shall be description of credit value of each module or unit in the course.
h) There shall be lesson's overview, content and activities, assignments to provide the learning opportunities for learner to master the content.
i) The course shall be designed to teach concepts and skills that the learner will retain throughout the study.
j) There shall be multiple learning paths for engaging the learner in active learning.
k) The content shall provide opportunities for learners to engage in high-order thinking, critical-reasoning activities and thinking in increasing by complex ways.
l) There shall be appropriate readability levels, written language assignments and mathematical requirements.
m) The course shall be easy to navigate.
n) There shall be declaration of textbooks, courseware, and online resources necessary to refer additionally to complete and master the course.
o) The Computer-based material shall satisfy the needs of learners with disabilities.

5. *Curriculum and Pedagogy: Quality Standards*

a) The curriculum objectives shall be consistent with the mission of the HEI.
b) There shall be involvement of all the stakeholders in the process of framing the curriculum objective.
c) The curriculum shall be designed by adopting University Grants Commission Model Curriculum and incorporating local or regional needs.

d) There shall be rationale for the appropriateness of the curriculum to the stage of learning.
e) There shall be linkages of the curriculum to previous and subsequent stages of learning.
f) There shall be such learning experiences which allow a diversity of methods (like learning from practice, opportunities for distributed and concentrated practice, learning with peers, learning in formal situations inside and outside the department, personal study, specific teacher inputs, etc).
g) The structure of curriculum shall be defined.
h) There shall be a complete strategy on teaching and learning methods.
i) There shall be a decision made on types of media content used.
j) There shall be a comprehensive decision on assessment and evaluation techniques.
k) The content shall be reliable and justify the learning outcome(s).
l) There shall be clear definition of intended outcomes of learning, benchmarked to identifiable stages of learning.
m) There shall be the use of reference points and expertise from outside the Higher Educational Institution, if required, in programme design and in the processes of programme development and approval.
n) There shall be relevance of curriculum to national competency requirement.
o) There shall be description of credit value of each module or unit in the course.

Guidelines on Preparation of Self Learning Material

Overview

1. Self-Learning Material is developed with the approach of self-explanatory, self-contained, self-directed, self-motivating and self-evaluating. The major challenge for the Open and Distance Learning system is near absence of the teacher. Therefore, it is very essential to pre-plan each of the activities. The learning material plays a vital role in this system and it includes Self-Learning Material in print and electronic form. A key challenge of Learning Material is ensuring that its writing is to be in a way that is engaging and which actively involves the learners. Another challenge of learning material is rapidly changing technology and deploying traditional teaching-learning methods through these technologies. Therefore, it is necessary to have the proper planning prior to development of the

learning material. During the planned period, the following points should be considered very carefully:

- backgrounds of learner and learning needs;
- learning experiences; and
- support and preparation in adapting to flexible learning.

2. Learning materials place much more emphasis on the processes of learning. Following are the major ingredients to be considered while developing the learning material by authors (in case of print material) and instructional designers (in case of e-learning material):
   (a) learning objectives
   (b) assessment of prior knowledge
   (e) learning activities
   (d) feedback of learning activities
   (e) examples and illustrations
   (t) self-assessment tests
   (g) summaries and key points
   (h) study tips.
3. The learning material should be developed with the constructivist approach and that should lay emphasis on real-world tasks, learner's choice of tasks or situations, case studies, collaborative learning tasks, opportunities for observing others, self-evaluation. The Higher Educational Institution may also adopt or procure the Learning Materials from expert agencies or consultant if it saves the time and cost without compromising on the quality.

Planning for Development of Learning Material

4. Due to the near absence of the teachers in the Open and Distance Learning mode, the learner has the opportunity to take the decision(s) at any point during the learning path. This may create disagreement between learner's perception and the objective of the learning material. Therefore, it is required to consider the following key points during planning for the development of learning material.
   (a) ***Learner Profile***: It is required to consider literacy level (including level of language proficiency), age group, information communication technology skills, aim of study, personal background and home situation, prior knowledge, prior skills, learning situations, etc.
   (b) ***Background:*** In Open and Distance Learning system, learner studies at his pace and not like face-to-face mode. Most of the learners are working professionals and they get time to study at their homes. If we add certain references which they cannot access at home, then it will create an obstacle in their learning.

Therefore, it is necessary to consider the accessibility of course resources and references at the place of learning.

(c) ***Learning Objectives and Outcome*:** It is required to define the learning objectives and outcomes prior to initiating the process for the learning material development. The learning objectives can be of terminal, intermediate or enabling nature. These learning objectives can be set at course, unit, or module level.

Group of Learning Material

5. Considering the principles of Open and Distance Learning mode of education, the programmes shall be accompanied with learning material or resources which shall comprise of self-learning material or e-learning material, e-books, practical book, students' handbook, question bank, assignment book, Audio Video material, programme guide, project manual, etc.

Standards of Self Learning Material (SLM) in Print Form

i. The Self Learning Material shall be developed as per the defined credit structure of the programme.
ii. The Self Learning Material shall involve the learner actively through various experience-based activities and assignments.
iii. The learner shall get the clear information about the structure of the programme and the course.
iv. There shall be a detailed learning map in the Self Learning Material for the learner so that she or he will be self-directed for completion of their studies.
v. The content of the Self Learning Material shall be developed with dialogue and personal system of writing method which will create a nature of interactivity in the Self Learning Material.
vi. The Self Learning Material shall encourage the learner to apply new knowledge and skills.
vii. There shall be clear definition of learning objectives and outcomes.
viii. The content shall be divided into small sections (blocks) and sub-sections (units and sub-units) for effective learning.
ix. Activities shall be included in each unit of the Self Learning Material.
x. There shall be assignments on each learning objective for self-assessment.
xi. The learner shall be directed through problem solving activities as applicable to the nature of the course.

Standards of Self Learning Material (SLM) in Non-print Form

6. The learners' perspective is an important aspect of quality assurance for e-learning. High-quality e-learning content should be designed by skilled content and instructional design professionals. Good instructional design will reflect best practices and research on teaching and learning. The key principles of designing e-learning content are: (1) consistent layout and design; (2) clear organisation and presentation of information; (3) consistent and easy-to-use navigation; and (4) aesthetically pleasing design and graphics. Thus, the standards of Self Learning Material in non-print form are as under:

i. The e-learning material shall be designed as per the credit structure of the online programme.
ii. The course shall be organised into units and lessons.
iii. There shall be description of unit overview along with objectives, activities, assignments and resources that frame the unit.
iv. Availability of a programme map and correlation matrix among the courses in the programme.
v. There shall be description of credit value of each module or unit in the course.
vi. There shall be clear guidelines on academic integrity and netiquette (internet etiquette) expectations regarding lesson activities, discussions and plagiarism.
vii. There shall be lesson overview, content and activities, assignments to provide the learning opportunities for learner to master the content.
viii. The course shall be designed to teach concepts and skills that the learner will retain throughout the study.
ix. There shall be multiple learning paths for engaging the learner in active learning.
x. The content shall provide opportunities for learners to engage in high-order thinking, critical-reasoning activities and thinking in increasing by complex ways.
xi. There shall be appropriate readability levels, written language assignments and mathematical requirements.
xii. The content shall provide for periodical feedback about the learner process.
xiii. The course shall be easy to navigate.
xiv. There shall be declaration of textbooks, courseware, and online resources necessary to refer additionally to complete and master the course.
xv. The content shall be accessible on various devices.
xvi. The e-learning material shall satisfy the needs of learners with disabilities.

Learner Support Centre

1. *General*

Open and Distance Learning (ODL) mode of Education consists of three levels of functioning which are located at the Head Quarters (HQ) of the Higher Educational Institutions, Regional Centres and Study Centres (SCs) or Learner Support Centres (LSCs) established within the territorial jurisdiction of the Higher Educational Institution as defined in the following Part. Planning, Designing and Preparation of Self Learning Material (SLM) for a learner who does not have any regular access to teachers is quite different than a textbook meant for classroom teaching, overall management of the processes of Admissions, Evaluation, and Declaration of Results, etc. are the main responsibilities of the Head Quarters of the

Higher Educational Institution and are discharged from the main campus. Under the direct management and control of the Higher Educational Institution, Regional Centres which are the second level of functioning, perform a dynamic operational link between the Head Quarter and the Study Centres (SCs) or Learner Support Centres (LSCs) which are the third level of Open and Distance Learning system and are important main contact points for access by the learners, responsive and facilitating information centres, arranging contact sessions and other operations like processing of assignments, etc. The Study Centres (SCs) or Learner Support Centres (LSCs) will also be established and managed directly by the Higher Educational Institution and not through any franchise or outsourced arrangement.

2. *Definition and Establishment of Learner Support Centre or Study Centre*

'Study Centre (SC) or Learner Support Centre (LSC)' means a Centre established, maintained or recognised by the Higher Education Institution for advising, counselling, vocational guidance, hands on experience, library services and providing interface between the teachers and the learners, rendering academic and any other related services and assistance, like field experience, laboratory for experimental work, Information Communication Technology facilities for operations and interaction with the learners, etc. for the benefit of the learners:

Provided that a Higher Educational Institution offering programmes in Open and Distance Learning mode shall, within six months from the date of notification of these Regulations, ensure that all Study Centre or Learner Support Centre are established only in a College or Institute affiliated to a recognised university (other than a private university) or a Government recognized Higher Educational Institution offering conventional mode programmes of equivalent level in the same broad areas under the relevant faculty such as faculty of sciences or social science or humanities or commerce or management, etc. and having all the necessary infrastructure and availability of appropriate number of qualified faculty not below the rank of qualified Assistant Professors of recognised colleges or institutes offering a similar programme for engaging theory contact sessions and supervising practical sessions in laboratory or field:

Provided that a Higher Educational Institution may establish a Special Learner Support Centre for imparting instruction to persons referred to in the Persons with Disabilities (Equal Opportunities, Protection of Rights and Full Participation) Act, 1995, the National Trust for Welfare of Persons with Autism, Cerebral Palsy, Mental Retardation and Multiple Disability Act, 1999 including the employees of Defence or Security Forces and jail inmates interested to study through the Open and Distance Learning mode. However, in case of programmes like those being developed by the Government for Skill Development or Lifelong Learning, the Study Centre or Learner Support Centre could be opened in Government institutions having capabilities for learner support services in the respective areas.

Any Study Centre or Learner Support Centre shall be established by the Higher Educational Institution after processing through the appropriate statutory bodies of the Higher Educational Institution. While processing such approvals it is mandatory to provide evidence of the preparedness for establishing Study Centres/ Learner Support Centres, providing learner support services, availability of the academic, other staff and qualified academic counsellors.

The Higher Educational Institution shall have a Standard Operating Procedure for the smooth functioning of the Study Centre or Learner Support Centre which will include all aspects of functions of the Study Centre or Learner Support Centre, monitoring mechanism of different services provided by the Centre, and it shall be mandatory for the Study Centre or Learner support Centre to maintain the learner data related to conduct of counselling sessions, evaluation of assignments and effective and online grievance redressal system, which should be monitored at the level of regional centre and Head Quarters.

List of the Study Centre or Learner Support Centre as approved by the respective Higher Educational Institution shall be submitted to the University Grants Commission at least 60 days in advance before operationalising the Study Centres or Learner Support Centres. The list of Study Centres or Learner Support Centres with details such as: Name with address of the institution where the centre is located, name of the coordinator with contact details, working hours and schedules for counselling sessions, infrastructure and other facilities available in the Study Centre or Learner Support Centre shall be displayed on the web portal of the Open and Distance Learning institution and the same information shall be made available in the printed prospectus for the information of the learners and other stakeholders.

In addition, a Higher Educational Institution should submit an undertaking to the Commission that the academic and instructional facilities at its Study Centres or Learner Support Centres meet all the conditions of these regulations and guidelines issued from time to time, and are commensurate with the number of academic programmes and learners-strength thereto:

Provided that the Higher Educational Institution shall not carry out any of its activities related to the Open and Distance Learning mode at places other than Study Centres or Learner Support Centres under a different name such as Information Centre, Facilitation Centre, Nodal Centre, Knowledge Partner, Partner Institution, Multimedia Centre and similar such names;

Provided further that, no Study Centre or Learner Support Centre shall be established beyond the jurisdiction of the Higher Educational Institution or under any franchisee or outsourcing agreement, as described in these regulations.

3. *Territorial Jurisdiction for Establishment of Study Centres or Learner Support Centres*

Territorial jurisdiction of the Higher Educational Institution for Open and Distance Learning mode programmes shall be as prescribed in the respective Acts of the Higher Educational Institution, subject to the following conditions:

3.1 *Higher Educational Institution other than Private and Deemed to be University*: Not beyond the respective State in case of universities set up under any State Act. For universities set up under a Central Act, the jurisdiction shall be as per the provisions of the Act.

3.2. *Deemed to be a University*: The jurisdiction shall be as per extant provisions of the Deemed to be a university regulations and also notified by the University Grants Commission from time to time.

3.3. *Private University:* A Private University established under a State Act shall be unitary in nature and will be eligible to run Open and Distance Learning Programmes, which have been conducted by the university in conventional mode for a minimum period of five years. The Learner Support Centres or Study Centres shall be set up, within the State, with the prior approval of the University Grants Commission and as per University Grants Commission (Establishment and Maintenance of Standards in Private Universities) Regulations, 2003. In the absence of University Grants Commission approved Learner Support Centre or Study Centre, the University shall offer distance education programmes at its main campus only.

4. Admission and Programme Fees

Admission of learners to a Higher Educational Institution for a programme in Open and Distance Learning mode shall be offered in a transparent manner with Self Learning Material designed and developed directly by the Higher Educational Institution which shall be solely responsible for all activities relating to admissions or registration or evaluation processes, duly approved by the respective statutory bodies of the Higher Educational Institutions. In no case these activities shall be outsourced. However, quality Self Learning Material developed by any other Higher Educational Institutions recognised by the University Grants Commission to run Open and Distance Learning programmes could be used under a mutual agreement after seeking approval of the University Grants Commission:

Provided that a Study Centre or Learner Support Centre shall not admit a learner to any programme in Open and Distance Learning mode for or on behalf of any other Higher Educational Institution.

Every Higher Educational institution shall publicise a prospectus on the web portal of the Higher Educational institutions before the expiry of sixty days prior to the date of commencement of admission to any of its programmes in the Open and Distance learning mode. Such a prospects shall contain the following information for learners seeking admission to any programme of the institution and for the general public:

i. each component of the fee and any other charges or deposits payable by the learners admitted to such Higher Educational Institutions for pursuing a programme in Open and Distance Learning mode, and clear terms and conditions of such payments to be charged by the Institute;
ii. the percentage of tuition fee and other charges refundable to a learner admitted in such Higher Educational Institutions in case such a learner withdraws from the institution before joining or after full completion of course or programme of study and the time within, and the manner in which such refund shall be made to the learner;
iii. the number of seats approved in respect of each course or programme of Open and Distance Learning mode;
iv. Eligibility conditions for admission including educational qualifications specified by the relevant statutory authority or

body, or by the institution, where no such qualifying standards have been specified by any statutory authority;

v. the process of admission and selection of eligible learners applying for such admission, including all relevant information in regard to the details of test or examination, if any, for selecting such candidates for admission to each course or programme of study and the amount of fee to be paid for the admission test;

vi. details of the academic faculty at the Headquarters or Regional Centres or Study Centre or Learner Support Centre, including therein the educational qualifications and experience in teaching or conduction of Open and Distance Learning programmes and also indicating therein whether such a faculty member is on regular basis or visiting or contract basis;

vii. the minimum pay and other emoluments payable for each category of faculty and Officers of the institute;

viii. physical and academic infrastructure and other facilities, including that of each of the Study Centre or Learner Support Centre and in particular the laboratory, library and Information and Communication Technology facilities to be provided to learners on being admitted to the institution; and

ix. broad outline of the syllabus specified by the appropriate statutory body or by institution, as the case may be, for every course or programme of study.

5. *Norms for Empanelment of Academic Counsellors and Counselling Sessions*

5.1. *Eligibility conditions for appointment of academic counsellors*: No academic staff in the Study Centre or Learner Support Centre shall be appointed who does not fulfill the minimum qualifications as laid down in the University Grants Commission (Minimum Qualifications for Appointment of Teachers and other Academic Staff in the Universities and Colleges and Measures for the Maintenance of Standards in Higher Education) Regulation, 2010 as modified from time to time. In addition, such academic staff should have familiarity with the characteristics of Open and Distance Learning mode learners and their needs, difference between Open and Distance Learning and conventional face to face education, awareness about instructional design, familiarity with the learner centered approach in blended mode of learning, ability to use different delivery media including online and computer mediated communication and Information and Communication Technology enabled learning.

5.2. *Norms for Contact Programmes*: Credit Based System has been followed by Open and Distance Learning single mode Higher

Educational Institutions during the last more than two decades and it has got standardised for programme delivery especially by the Open Universities. Such credits depend on the total number of hours that a learner is required to cover for all activities like participation in contact programmes, Working on Assignments, Library Consultation, etc., in completing a course. In this direction, University Grants Commission has recently issued guidelines for introduction of Choice Based Credit System (CBCS) which has been made mandatory for all Higher Educational Institutions delivering education through conventional mode. Accordingly, for Post Graduate programmes in Open and Distance Learning mode, 16 credits per semester are assigned for a total of four semesters. In Open and Distance Learning mode programme delivery, the component of contact with teachers is comparatively much lower than the conventional or face to face mode which is complemented by self-learning on the part of the learner. Therefore, one credit in regular or face to face mode accounts for 15 teaching hours, whereas, in Open and Distance Learning mode it is 30 study hours of study including face to face contact component. Comparative credits assigned per semester in Choice Based Credit System for conventional mode and Open and Distance Learning mode for undergraduate programmes is given below.

Monitoring of functioning of the Learner Support Centres or Study Centres

Generally, the Open and Distance Learning mode Higher Educational Institutions have to manage a fairly large and well spread system with a variety of learner centric operations for a number of heterogeneous groups of learners to meet their expectations and self-learning requirements using multimode programme delivery. To effectively manage these challenges and complex operations for a learner at a distance, a very dynamic interactive communication system between Headquarters, regional centres and study centres has to be established on priority. Thus, it is desirable that an Information and Communication Technology network connecting the Head Quarters, Regional Centres and Study Centre or Learner Support Centres should be established at the earliest and used for faster and reliable operations such as:

i. username and login ID should be generated for every learner so that learners can see all relevant information as their studies progress in an Open and Distance Learning programme and also provide constructive feedback for improvement in Open and Distance Learning programme delivery;
ii. head quarters, regional centres and study centre or learner support centres should maintain a web portal giving all

relevant information about the Open and Distance Learning programmes being a delivered and the content of these should be updated at least on a weekly basis;

iii. regional centres should collect a holistic report about all functions assigned to study centres or learner support centres and all aspects of quality of programme delivery periodically especially during the admissions, examinations, and counselling sessions etc., and at least weekly share a consolidated report with the head quarters;

iv. these reports along with responses by learners should be periodically analysed for the quality audit of a programme and its delivery besides the quality of performance of the study centres or learner support centres;

v. any remedial action should be jointly ensured by the head quarters, regional centres and study centres or learner support centres promptly;

vi. Regular visits, at least twice a year by the academic staff of the Higher Educational Institution for on the spot monitoring and interaction with functionaries of the regional centres and study centres or learner support centres, the learners and the counsellors, and

vii. Ensuring access of "Swayam" and other repositories of Massive Open Online Courses by the learners at study centres or learner support centres.

Closure of Non-performing Study Centre or Learner Support Centre

In case a study centre or learner support centre fails to adhere to the prescribed norms or guidelines, the Higher Educational Institution shall initiate action for closure of the centre by following due procedures, so that interest of learners are taken care of by some alternative arrangement.

Grievance Redressal Mechanism

Scope of Grievance Redressal System for Learner

The Higher Educational Institutions, offering programmes through the Open and Distance Learning mode, shall have a Grievance Redressal System and Procedure which shall be published on the portal of Higher Educational Institution and it shall be the responsibility of the concerned Higher Educational Institution to update the same as and when required. Each of the Higher Educational Institutions shall provide an online facility for submitting grievances and track their status. The Higher

Educational Institution shall also be responsible for monitoring, assessing and reviewing the effectiveness of its Grievance Redressal Procedures.

Guidelines and Standards for the Grievance Redressal System

The Higher Educational Institution shall have the policy on Grievance Redressal System based on following guidelines and standards, namely:

a) the policy should be unbiased and understandable;
b) there should be a time line for each stage of the process;
c) the policy should be published on Higher Educational Institutions portal so that the learners may read and refer to;
d) the policy should be made available to learners with disability in appropriate format and the provision should be made accordingly in the policy document;
e) the authority or authorities involved in the grievance redressal process should treat and investigate facts impartially;
f) the Higher Educational Institutions should address the grievances in a timely manner so as to lessen interruption in learning process of the learner. The Higher Educational Institution should have the proper communication and escalation mechanism which can be operated and maintained through the online software application;
g) the Higher Educational Institution should maintain the confidentiality of the complainant as far as possible;
h) the Higher Educational Institution should ensure that officer(s) deputed for the learner support at the Higher Educational Institution, the Regional Centres and Learner Support Centre(s) are able to provide guidance on submitting grievances in the portal;
i) There should be a provision to withdraw a complaint without prejudice at any time during the procedure; and
j) The learner should be kept informed of the status in relation to his queries or grievance on priority.

Rights and Responsibilities of a Learner

a) The learner has the right to complain regarding any aspect related to his or her learning path including programme quality, learning resources, learner support and guidance, teaching, learning and assessment.
b) The learner is entitled to approach the respective Learner Support Centres (in case of offline or blended learning) for submitting his or her complaint. The learners of online mode

may submit their complaint directly to the Higher Educational Institution. The complaint can be submitted individually or collectively by a group of learners.

c) The learner should submit a formal complaint in a manner prescribed by the Higher Educational Institution regarding expression of dissatisfaction with a service provided or the lack of a service or the quality of a service. Such expression should be correlated with what the learners were entitled to receive.

Responsibility of the Higher Educational Institution

i. The Higher Educational Institution shall work with the principles of openness and collaboration.

ii. The Higher Educational Institution shall continuously improve the services it offers. As and when a grievance is received, the Higher Educational Institution shall investigate it thoroughly and make the necessary improvement(s) in its services.

iii. The Higher Educational Institution shall encourage Learner Support Centres to make initial attempts to address and resolve complaints as close as possible to the point of origin, and with the minimum of formality.

iv. The Higher Educational Institution shall also monitor the Grievance Redressal process through its Learner Support Centres.

v. The Higher Educational Institution is responsible for privacy and confidentiality unless disclosure is necessary to proceed in the matter.

vi. The grievance should be accompanied with the reasons for dissatisfaction and expected remedy. The learner should also give the reference of Online Grievance Registration Number generated at the time of submitting the complaint at the Learner Support Centre.

vii. The Head of concerned school of the Higher Educational Institution shall investigate the complaint(s) or refer the matter(s) to a more appropriate person, body or committee or departments, as appropriate.

viii. It shall be the responsibility of the Head of school of the Higher Educational Institution to monitor the progress and to timely resolve the matter.

ix. The Head of concerned school of the Higher Educational Institution will respond in writing (letters or email, etc.) through offline or online mode giving reasons for a decision and action taken thereto.

APPENDIX 1

List of Distance Education Institutions

Andhra Pradesh

- Acharya Nagarjuna University, Guntur
- Andhra University, Visakhapatnam
- Dr. B.R. Ambedkar Open University, Hyderabad
- Dravidian University, Kuppam
- Gitam University, Visakhapatnam
- Jawaharlal Nehru Technological University, Hyderabad
- Kakatiya University, Warangal
- Maulana Azad National Urdu University, Hyderabad
- NALSAR University of Law, Hyderabad
- Osmania University, Hyderabad
- Potti Sreeramulu Telugu University, Hyderabad
- Rashtriya Sanskrit Vidyapeetha, Tirupati
- Rayalseema University, Kurnool
- Sri Krishnadevaraya University, Anantapur
- Sri Padmavati Mahila Visvavidyalayam, Tirupati
- Sri Venkateswara University, Tirupati
- University of English and Foreign Languages, Hyderabad
- I CFAI Foundation for Higher Education, Hyderabad
- National Institute of Rural Development, Hyderabad

Arunachal Pradesh

- Rajiv Gandhi University, Itanagar

Assam

- Dibrugarh University, Dibrugarh
- Guwahati University, Guwahati
- Krishna Kanta Handique State Open University, Guwahati
- Don Bosco University Global, Guwahati
- Assam University, Silchar
- Assam Down Town University, Guwahati
- Tezpur University, Tezpur

Bihar

- Babasaheb Bhim Rao Ambedkar Bihar University, Muzaffarpur
- Lalit Narayan Mithila University, Darbhanga
- Magadh University, Bodh Gaya

- Nalanda Open University, Patna
- Patna University, Patna
- Jai University, Chhapra

Chhattisgarh

- Dr. CV Raman University, Bilaspur
- MATS University, Raipur
- Pt. Ravi Shankar Shukla University, Raipur
- Pandit Sundarlal Sharma (Open) University, Bilaspur

Delhi

- AIMA, Delhi
- Delhi University, Delhi
- Guru Gobind Singh Indraprastha University, Delhi
- Indira Gandhi National Open University, Delhi
- Institute of Rail Transport, New Delhi
- Jamia Hamdard, New Delhi
- Jamia Milia Islamia, New Delhi
- Rashtriya Sanskrit Sansthan, New Delhi
- TECNIA Institute of Technology, Delhi
- TERI School of Advanced Studies, New Delhi
- Institute of Management and Development. New Delhi
- National Institute of Health and Family Welfare, New Delhi

Gujarat

- Dr. Babasaheb Ambedkar Open University, Ahmedabad_
- Gujarat Vidyapith, Ahmedabad
- Sumandeep Vidyapeeth University, Vadodara
- Entrepreneurship Development institute of India. Ahmedabad
- Saurashtra University Rajkot

Haryana

- Chaudhary Devilal University, Sirsa
- Guru Jambheshwar University, Hisar
- JK Business School, Gurgaon, Haryana
- Kurukshetra University, Kurukshetra
- Maharishi Dayanandn University, Rohtak
- Maharshia Markandeshwar University, Amblala
- Manav Rachna International University
- IILM Institute of Higher Education, Gurgaon

Himachal Pradesh

- Himachal Pradesh University, Shimla

Jammu & Kasmir

- University of Jammu, Jammu
- University of Kashmir, Srinagar

Karnataka

- Gulbarga University, Gulbarga
- Kannada University, Hampi
- Karnataka University. Dharwad
- Kuvempu University, Shimoga
- Mangalore University, Mangalore
- National Law School of India University, Bangalore
- Visvesvaraya Technological University, Belgaum
- Bangalore University, Bangalore
- Manipal University, Manipal [Formerly Manipal Academy of Higher Education]
- Bhartiya Vidya Foundation, International School of Business and Research, Bangalore
- Karnataka State Women's University, Bijapur
- Tumkur University, Tumkur
- IFIM, Business School, Bangalore

Kerala

- Kannur University, Kannur
- Mahatma Gandhi University, Kottayam
- University of Calicut, Kozhikode
- University of Kerala. Thiruvananthapuram

Madhya Pradesh

- Awadhes Pratap Sing University, Rewa
- Barkatullah Vishwavidyalaya, Bhopal
- Devi Ahilya Vishwavidyalaya, Indore
- Dr. Harisingh Gour Vishwavidyalaya, Sagar
- Jiwaji University, Gwalior
- M.G . Chitrakoot Gramodaya Vishwavidyalaya, Chitrakoot
- Madhya Pradesh Bhoj Open University, Bhopal
- Maharishi Mahesh Yogi Vedic Vishwavidyalaya, Katni
- Rani Durgawati University, Jabalpur

Maharashtra

- Bharati Vidyapeeth University, Pune
- Dr. D Y Patil University, Pune
- Indian Institute of Material Management, Navi Mumbai
- Indian School of Business Management and Administration

- Indira International Distance Education Academy, IGI, Pune
- International Institute for Population Sciences, Mumbai
- Mahatma Gandhi Antarrashtriya Hindi Vishwavidyalaya, Wardha
- NMIMS University, Mumbai
- Padmashree Dr. DY Patil University, Navi Mumbai
- Sant Gadge Baba Amravati University, Amravati
- Shivaji University, Kolhapur
- Shreemati Nathibai Daodar Thackersey (SNDT) Women's University, Mumbai
- Sinhgad Technical Education Society, Pune
- Swami Ramanand Teerth Marathwada University, Nanded
- Symbiosis Centre for Distance Learning, Pune
- Tata Institute of Social Sciences, Mumbai
- Tilak Maharashtra Vidyapeeth, Pune
- University of Mumbai, Mumbai
- Welingkar Institute of Management Studies, Mumbai
- Yashwantrao Chavan Maharashtra Open University, Nashik
- Balaji Institute of Modern Management, Pune
- Mumbai Education Trust, Mumbai
- Rashtrabhasha Prachar Samiti, Wardha
- MIT School of Distance Education, Pune
- PSB Educational Foundation, Pune

Meghalaya

- Mahatma Gandhi University, Khana Para
- NEHU, Shillong

Mizoram

- ICFAI, Aizawl

Nagaland

- The Global Open University, Dimapur

Odisha

- Asian School of Business Management, Bhubaneswar
- Berhampur University, Berhampur
- Fakir Mohan University, Balasore
- North Orissa University, Mayurbhanj
- Sambalpur University, Sambalpur
- Odisha State Open University, Sambalpur
- Utkal University, Bhubaneswar

Puducherry

- Pondicherry University, Puducherry

Punjab

- Guru Nanak Dev University, Amritsar
- Lovely Professional University, Phagwara
- Punjab University, Chandigarh
- Punjab Technical University, Jalandhar
- Punjabi University, Patiala
- Thapar University, Patiala

Rajasthan

- Bhagwant University, Ajmer
- Jagan Nath University, Jaipur
- Jain Vishva Bharati Institute, Ladnun
- Jaipur National University, Jaipur
- Jayoti Vidyapeeth Women's University, Jaipur
- JRN Rajasthan Vidyapeeth, Udaipur
- NIMS University, Jaipur
- Vardhman Mahaveer Open University, Kota
- Institute of Advance Studies in Education, Sardarshahar
- Birla Institute of Technology and Sciences, Pilani
- Suresh Gyan Vihar University, Jaipur
- Jodhpur National University, Jodhpur

Sikkim

- ICFAI University, Gangtok
- Sikkim Manipal University, Gangtok
- EIILM University, Jorethang
- Vinayaka Mission's Sikkim University, Gangtok

Tamil Nadu

- Alagappa University, Karaikudi
- Annamalai University, Annamalainagar
- Bharathiar University, Coimbatore
- Bharathidasan University, Tiruchirapalli
- Karpagam University, Coimbatore
- Madurai Kamaraj University, Madurai
- Manonmaniam Sundaranar University, Tirunelveli
- Meenakshi Academy of Higher Education and Research
- Meenakshi University, Chennai
- Mother Teresa Women's University, Kodaikanal
- Periyar University, Salem
- St. Peter's University, Chennai
- Tamil Nadu Agricultural University, Coimbatore
- Tamil Nadu Dr. Ambedkar Law University, Chennai
- Tamil Nadu Open University, Chennai

- Tamil University, Thanjavur
- University of Madras, Chennai
- Vinayaka Missions University, Salem
- Bharath Institute of Higher Education and Research, Chennai
- Gandhigram Rural Institute, Gandhigram
- Shanmugha Arts Science, Technology and Research Academy, Thanjavur
- Sri Chandrasekharendra Saraswathi Viswamahavidyalaya, Kanchipuram
- Sri Ramachandra University, Chennai
- Ponnaiyah Ramajayam Institute of Science and Technology, Thanjavur
- Periyar Maniammai University, Thanjavur
- Karunya Institute of Technology and Sciences, Coimbatore
- Confederation of Indian Industry of Logistics, Chennai

Tripura

- ICFAI University, Agartala
- Tripura University, Agartala

Uttarakhand

- Dev Sanskriti Vishwavidyalaya, Haridwar
- ICFAI University, Dehradun
- University of Petroleum and Energy Studies, Dehradun
- Uttarakhand Open University, Haldwani
- Kumaun University, Nainital
- Gurukul Kangri Vishwavidyalaya, Haridwar

Uttar Pradesh

- Aligarh Muslim University, Aligarh
- Amity University, Noida
- Dayalbagh Education Institute, Agra
- IMT Distance and Learning Institution, Ghaziabad
- Indian Institute of Carpet Technology, Bhadohi
- IMT, Greater Noida
- Shobhit University, Modipuram
- Swami Vivekananda Subharti University, Meerut
- Uttar Pradesh Rajarshi Tandon Open University
- University of Allahabad, Allahabad
- Sam Higginbottom Institute of Agriculture, Technology and Sciences, (Deemed University), Allahabad [Formerly, Allahabad Agricultural Institute]
- Dr. B.R. Ambedkar University, Agra
- Jagadguru Rambhadracharya Handicapped University, Chitrakoot
- BLS Institute of Management, Ghaziabad

- NIMT Institute of Technology and Management, Ghaziabad
- Teerthankar Mahaveer University, Moradabad
- Integral University, Lucknow
- Graduate School of Business and Administration, Greater Noida

West Bengal

- Jadavpur University, Kolkata
- Netaji Subhas Open University, Kolkata
- Rabindra Bharati University, Kolkata
- University of Burdwan, Burdwan
- University of Kalyani, Kalyani
- University of North Bengal, Darjeeling
- Vidyasagar University, Midnapore

APPENDIX 2

Open Universities

	Open Universities in India	*Year of Establishment*
1.	Dr. B.R. Ambedkar Open University, Hyderabad	1982
2.	Indira Gandhi National Open University, Delhi	1985
3.	Vardhman Mahaveer Open University, Kota, Rajasthan	1987
4.	Nalanda Open University, Patna, Bihar	1987
5.	Yashwant Chavan Maharashtra Open University, Nashik, Maharashtra	1989
6.	Madhya Pradesh Bhoj Open University, Bhopal, Madhya Pradesh	1991
7.	Dr Baba Saheb Ambedkar Open University, Ahmedabad, Gujarat	1994
8.	Karnataka State Open University, Mysore, Karnataka	1996
9.	Netaji Subhash Open University, Kolkata, West Bengal	1997
10.	Uttar Pradesh Raj Rishi Tandon Open University, Allahabad, Uttar Pradesh	1998
11.	Tamil Nadu Open University, Chennai, Tamil Nadu	2002
12.	Pandit Sundarlal Sharma Open University, Raipur, Chhatisgarh	2005
13.	The Global Open University, Nagaland	2006
14.	K. K. Handique Open University, Guwahati, Assam	2007
15.	Uttarkhand Open University, Dehradun, Uttarakhand	2007
16.	Venkateshwara Open University, Lekhi, Arunachal Pradesh	2012
17.	Odisha State Open University, Sambalpur, Odisha	2016

APPENDIX 3

Subjects in which Distance Courses are Offered

Agriculture Science
Aviation Management
Air Hostess Training
Accountancy
Advertising and Public Relations
Banking
Business Studies
Business Management
BBA
BGL
BCA
Bioinformatics
Biotechnology
Botany
Coastal Aquaculture
Clinical Research
Commerce
Computerised Accounting
Cooperation and Rural Studies
Catering Science
Chemical Engineering
Civil Engineering
Child Care and Education
Corporate Securities Law
Cyber Law
Costume Design
Computer Applications
Computer Science
Chemistry
Dairy Technology
Diabetology
Disaster Management
Design Management
E-Business
Entrepreneurship
Export Management
Electrical and Electronic Engineering
Electrical and Communication Engineering
Education Management
Education Technology
Elementary Teacher Training
Environment Science
Economics
English
Food and Beverage Services
Finance
Financial Planning
Financial Management
Front Office Management
Fashion Design
Fine Arts
Graphic Design
Herbal Science
Health and Fitness
Health Science
Hospital Management

Hindi
History
Human Rights
Human Resource Management
Hotel Management
House Keeping Management
International Business
Information System Management
Insurance Management
Industries Automation
Interior Design
Information Technology
Information Systems
Journalism and Mass Communication
Labour Laws
LLM
Library Science
Marketing Management
Mechanical Engineering
MCA
Mathematics
Microbiology
Networking
Office Automation
Paramedical Science
Philosophy
Political Science
Psychology
Public Administration
Personnel Management and Industrial Relations
Police Administration
Physical Education
Physics
Pharmaceutical Management
Public Health
Poultry Management
Retail Management
Rural Management
Sanskrit
Social work
Sociology
Secretaryship
Sports Management
Software Engineering
Telecom Management
Telugu
Tamil
Taxation Laws
Travel and Tourism
Ultrasonography and Medical Imaging
Yoga
Zoology

References

Bates, A.W. (2005), *Technology, E-Learning and Distance Education.* London: Routledge

Basu, S.(2015), Are Open Universities facing an identity crisis? *University News*, 53(6).

Basu, S. and Srinivasa, M. (2012), Looking Beyond Conventional Wisdom: Need for National Policy on ODL, *University News*, 50 (27)

CEMCA. (2015), *Status of the State Open Universities in India: Report.* New Delhi: CEM CA-COL

Government of AP (1982), *Towards an Open Learning system: Report of the Committee on the Establishment of an Open University*. Hyderabad: Govt. of AP

Government of India (1975), *Report of the Working Group on National Open University*. New Delhi: Govt. of India.

Gupta, Arun and Renu Arun (1986), Survey of Recent Indian Writings in Distance Education *Distance Education*, 1 (2)

Government of India. (2011), *Report of the Committee to Suggest Measures to Regulate the Standards of Education Being Imparted through Distance Mode*. Chairman: NR. Madhava Menon

Harry, K. (1999), *Higher Education through Open and Distance Learning.* London: Routledge

Halmberg, B. (1995), *Theory and Practice of Distance Education*

Koul, L. (2006), Research in Indian Distance Education. In Garg. S, Venkaiah, V., Puranik , C. Panda, SK. (eds). *Four Decades of Distance Education in India: Reflections on Policy and Practice.* New Delhi: Viva

Koul, L. (1997), Open and Distance Education. *Fifth Survey of Education Research* (1988-92) Trend Report. New Delhi: NCERT

Keegan, D. (1990), *Foundations of Distance Education*. London: Routledge

Kulandai Swamy, V.C. (1995), Social Demand for Higher Education in Asia: How Cost Effective are Open Universities. *Indian Journal of Open Learning.*

Kulandai Swamy, V.C. (1997), *Dr. BRAOU: The Next Decade- A Vision- A Study:* Commissioned by COL

Manjulika, S and Reddy, V. (1999), *Unexplored Dimensions of Open Universities*. New Delhi: Vikas

Manjulika, S and Reddy, V. (1996), *Distance Education in India: A Model for Developing Countries*. New Delhi: Vikas

Mishra, S. (1997), A critical Analysis of Periodical Literature in Distance Education. *Indian Journal of Open Learning,* 6 (1)

Mugridge, I. (1997), *Foundation the Open Universities: Essays in Memory of G. Ram Reddy.* New Delhi: Sterling

Murali Manohar, K., Sudhakar, G., Rajendra Prasad, D. (1996), *Distance Education Research in India: A Bibliometric Study.* Warangal: IDEA

Mishra, S. (1998), Distance Education Research: A Review of Its Structure, Methodological Issues and Priority Areas. *Indian Journal of Open Learning*, 7 (3).

Nembiakkim, R and Mishra, S. (2010), Research in Distance Education Attitudes and Barriers. *Indian Journal of Open Learning*, 19 (3)

National Knowledge Commission (2009) *Report to the Nation*, (2006-09) New Delhi.

Nageshwar Rao, (2017), *Learner Centric Open and Distance Learning System-Trends and Concerns (2017 Foundation Day Lecture, BRAOU).* Hyderabad: BRAOU

Panda, S.K. (ed). (1999), *Open and Distance Education.* New Delhi: Aravalli

Panda, S.K. (1995). Review of Research in India Distance Education. *Journal of Higher Education*, 8 (3)

Pandal, S.K., (1992), Distance Educational Research in India. Stock Taking, Concerns and Prospects. *Distance Education*, 13 (2)

Panda, S.K. Satyanarayana, P., and Sharma, R.C. (1996), *Open and Distance Education Research: Analysis and Annotation.* Warangal: IDEA

Prasad, V.S. and Venkaiah, V. (2005), *India's First Open University: Experiences of Two Decades*. Hyderabad: BRAOU

Report of the Committee on Correspondence Courses. New Delhi: 1986

Rumble, G and Harry, K. (ed) (1982), *The Distance Teaching Universities.* London: Croom Helm

Ram Reddy, G. (1992), *Open Universities: The Ivory Towers Thrown Open*. New Delhi: Sterling

Ram Reddy, G. (1987), Planning and Management and Monitoring of Distance Education. In *Distance Education in Asia and Pacific, Vol-I*. Manila: ADB

Rajagopalan, T. (2007), *Study of the Development of the State Open Universities in India*. Vancouver: COL

Satyanarayana, P. and Sesharatnam, C. (2000), *Distance Education: What? Why? How?* Hyderabad: Book Links

Satyanarayana, P., Saharatnam, C., Emmanuel, D.K. Meduri: (2015) *Distance Education: Origin, Growth and Development*: Delhi: Shipra Publication, New Delhi

Satyanarayana, P. and Raghunath, R. (1991), Research in Distance Education: A Bird's Eye View. *ICDE Bulletin*, 27

Satyanarana, P. (1995), *India's Educational Research: Contours and Concerns.* Hyderabad: IGNOU

Sanjay Tiwari (2017), Framework for Ranking of Distance Education Institutes in India: A Suggestive Model. *University News*. 53 (8)

Sahoo, P.K. (1993), *Higher Education at a Distance*. New Delhi: Sanchar

Sahoo, P.K. (1998), Research in Distance Education at University Level in India. *Media and Technology for Human Resource Development*, 2 (1)

Singh, B. (1992), *Correspondence/ Distance Education in India. An in depth Study*, New Delhi: IGNOU

Sujatha, K. (1988), Research on Distance Education in India. *Indian Journal of Distance Education,* 2

Sesharatnam, C. (1994), *Multimedia International System in Distance Education: A Case Study of DRAOU. (Ph.D Thesis).* Hyderabad: Osmania University

Sesharatnam, C. (1996), *Research in Distance Education in A.P. In M.S. Rao (ed). Synergy-Facets of Research in Open Learning* Hyderabad: BRAOU

Sesharatnam, C. (2002), *India's First Open University: Two Decades Journey.* Hyderabad: Booklinks.

Srivastava, M. (2012), *Open Universities: India's Answer to Challenges in Higher Education.* New Delhi: Vikas

Srivastava, M, and Rao, D. (2015), Restructuring of Indian Open Universities: Need of the Hour. *University News, 53(2)*

UGC (1984), Report of the Committee to Enquire into the Working of Central Universities. New Delhi: UGC

Usha V. Reddi and Mishra, S. (2005), *Educational Media in Asia.* Vancouver: COL

Venkaiah, V. (2002), *Teaching and Instructional Strategies in Open and Distance Learning.* New Delhi: AAOU

Yash Pal Committee (2009), *Report of the Committee to Advise on Renovation and Rejuvenation of Higher Education.* New Delhi.

Index